20830 (2)

SOME PRINCIPLES OF FICTION

SOME PRINCIPLES OF
FICTION

ROBERT LIDDELL

JONATHAN CAPE

THIRTY BEDFORD SQUARE   LONDON

FIRST PUBLISHED 1953
REPRINTED . 1956
REPRINTED . 1961

PRINTED IN GREAT BRITAIN BY
LOWE AND BRYDONE (PRINTERS) LTD., LONDON, N.W.10
BOUND BY A. W. BAIN & CO. LTD., LONDON

CONTENTS

5

CONTENTS

IV. DIALOGUE

V. TERMS AND TOPICS

CONTENTS

'INTIMATIONS OF IMMORTALITY'

7

APOLOGY

Any general examination of the novelist's art must appear arid and theoretical. It cannot fail to be directed towards the more formal elements in that art, while criticism of individual novelists can deal more adequately with the life they are trying to create. A book of this sort is doomed to appear excessively schematic, and some people may object that profitable things can be said about this or that novel, but hardly about the Novel; for as Lawrence said: 'all rules of construction hold good only for novels that are copies of other novels'.

That a great many things cannot be said in a book of this sort must be obvious to anyone who has ever given any thought to the novel. One can isolate for the purpose of analysis such an element as Plot, for instance — but in many novels that do not lack unity, the principle of cohesion is something we cannot call Plot, something to which we cannot do justice except in individual studies of these books or of their authors.

But though much must be left unsaid, something can be said — and a generalization may be useful even if it does not cover every instance. One of the purposes of such an examination is to help writers; and it is very difficult indeed to help writers except over formal problems. The only useful help many writers have ever given or received has been over small points such as punctuation, or the phrasing of a sentence.

The present book deals with other aspects of the novel than those dealt with in my former treatise. It aspires only to an internal consistency. It is not a correction or a defence or a completion of the former book, but has an independent existence of its own. If anything said here implies a slightly different view from that expressed in the first book (and this must sometimes be the case), I have not thought it required mention.

I

THE SUBJECT OF FICTION

§1. THE DIFFICULTY OF CHOOSING A SUBJECT AT THE PRESENT DAY

There is, no doubt, too much written and said about the present day, too much speculation about what the novelist *must* do to-day, and will *have* to do tomorrow. In the arts it is not very important to be up-to-date, and nothing looks more out-of-date today than the book that was up-to-date a year or two ago. And it is not an intelligent exercise to ask such questions as: 'What is the future of the novel?' or: 'Has the novel a future?'

A very few words on this point should be enough. While English remains a living language, in which prose can be read and written fluently, and so long as people live, and there are personal relations between them — then English fiction is possible. Reasons may make it more difficult to write at one time than another — it is probably now, for several reasons, as difficult as it has been at any time since the life-time of Richardson. It is especially difficult to find a suitable subject.

§2. THE INSECURITY OF LIFE

The chief difficulty today is caused by the crushing impact of public affairs. 'There is no private life which has not been determined by a wider public life,' says George Eliot — but since her day the determination has been very much more rigid. No one in Middlemarch, after all, ever had to join the armed forces, ever had to leave Middlemarch if he did not like it. And those who remained in Middlemarch never had to fear that their lives might be cut short or their homes destroyed by a bomb.

Nowadays, if a hero and heroine marry at the end of a book, and live happily ever afterwards — although we know that fictional characters are only puppets, and that the toy-box is shut at the end of the book, yet we cannot help asking how long that happiness is likely to last. Writer and reader alike feel an insecurity: we only half believe in the happiness or un-happiness of real persons, and therefore of fictional characters which are their *simulacra* — it seems such a frail thing.

On the other hand, if we read one of those bluff, middlebrow writers who seem to pride themselves on having escaped the jaded nerves of our epoch — then we believe even less in the characters or in the world that they have created. They seem to have been incapable of sensitively imagining what it is like to be alive today.

Already, after the first world war, Katherine Mansfield was complaining of writers who wrote as if it had not occurred. 'I don't want (God forbid!) mobilization and the violation of Belgium, but the novel can't just leave the war out. There must have been a change of heart.'[1]

Today we do not ask for pages about the Spanish war (God forbid!) or the Munich agreement — which loom too large as it is in contemporary fiction.

What we do demand of an author is rather, perhaps, a feeling of sadness, a lack of faith in simple or easy solutions to human problems, a sense of the frailty of life . . . no loud, hearty songs of innocence, but quiet songs of experience; and a great part of the experience of our time is expressed in a few, sad little words of Mr. Stephen Spender's:

THE INSECURITY OF LIFE

Who live under the shadow of a war,
What can I do that matters?

There is no attempt here to lay a moral or social duty upon the writer; it is an attempt to define an artistic duty for the novelist who is trying in any way to represent contemporary life. One can hardly write truthfully about characters living in this age without showing that many of them live in perpetual fear that their world is in imminent danger of falling to pieces round their ears. It would be like writing a novel about the Middle Ages, and leaving out the fear of Hell. This is not to suggest that the novelist could or should have a scheme for saving the world; if he thinks he knows how to save the world, then he had better go to work about it, and leave off writing fiction, for fiction will not hold the world together. Nor do we much want to read the views of his characters upon public events, for they will be very stale by the time the book is in print. We only require sadness, scepticism and a feeling of insecurity.

Those novels which people used to write at one time, about consumptive patients in sanatoria, would not be a bad model for present-day novelists, if they were better novels — for all characters nowadays are sick, with 'this strange disease of modern life', and it will probably carry them off. Whether characters are, for example, *Munichois* or *anti-Munichois* is only a question of which way they have got the disease: we do not want to know, for clinical details are boring.

In this unfortunate age in which we live, since everything is insecure, some people think it does not much matter how they behave — these people become criminals. Others, less extreme in their application of a similar point-of-view, still think that it does not very much matter what any individual does or suffers:

these people are apt to be impatient with fiction. What can it matter, they argue, what an imaginary person does or suffers, when the world's fate hangs in the balance? Are not novelists fiddling while Rome is burning?

This is not so sensible an attitude as it might at first appear. The fate of the world, after all, is only important in so far as it affects the people in it. We may speak, if we like, of Poland, Spain or wherever suffering; but of course it means nothing: it is only Poles, Spaniards or whoever that can suffer. Moreover we cannot even say that two Poles, for example, can suffer twice as much as one. Suffering is not a thing that can be added up or multiplied, like horsepower. There is never more suffering, or worse suffering at any one time in the world than the worst that can be contained in one human consciousness.

If we think that it does not matter what happens to the individual, then we have no reason to think that it matters what happens to the world, for it is the individual who feels what happens to the world.

If we think the individual matters, then our sympathy can as easily be extended to the imaginary individual — for other people are to us for the most part imaginary individuals. And if the novelist seems to be fiddling while Rome is burning, it may be a useful service to play to the firemen while they have their luncheon.

St. Augustine says that he could not weep for his sins, which might plunge him into Hell, but he could weep for Dido's unhappy love. He thought this a sign of his own perversity, but we may also regard it as a sign of Vergil's artistry: Vergil made him weep for Dido. A novelist may still hope to make us weep for his heroine, and to forget for a while the things that may plunge us in ruin; but his Dido, if she is a woman living in the world of today, will have a shakier throne to sit on, and a more unstable background than that of the Queen of Carthage. This is one of the things that will make her story more difficult to tell. The novelist not only has to keep his eye on his character, and no interesting characters keep still for very long — he has also to keep his eye upon a surrounding world that will not keep still, as it kept (comparatively) still for Jane Austen or for Trollope — to see steadily what is, itself, unsteady.

§ 3. THE STANDARDIZATION OF LIFE

Not only is life insecure, it may also be said that it is less interesting than it used to be, and that people are not so interesting as they used to be. When people profess to find that Dickens's characters are wild exaggerations, and when they say that they have never seen anyone remotely like Mrs. Gamp or Mr. Pecksniff, it is to be feared that they are often telling the truth — they haven't. Those of us who have been more fortunate, must sorrowfully admit that the most Dickensian people of our acquaintance are now elderly, or in their graves.

The standardization of life, alas, requires no proof. The progress of machinery has made the working-lives of industrial labourers infinitely less interesting, as everyone knows. It may be possible to avoid the uglification of life — well-designed things can be made by machines; it may be possible, by use of machinery, so to cut down working hours that industrial labourers may (on the balance) be happier. This is no consolation to the novelist as such, who does not care whether they are happy or not, or whether what they make is beautiful or hideous. He would like their working-lives to be interesting and significant as a subject for fiction — and that they will never be again. If we look, on the contrary, at the lives of stone-masons or woodlanders in the Wessex novels, we can see at once how rich their working-lives were in material for the novelist.

Again, big businesses, multiple stores and the like may be able to do much for their work-people, but one thing they cannot give them, an interesting working-life. Yet for anyone who had worked for Mrs. Todgers or for Poll Sweedlepipe or for any of the little shops and businesses in Dickens, life would have been full of drama.

The standardization of life does not only blight people's working-lives, but also their amusements. A big household, like that of Mansfield Park, would be unlikely today to get up private theatricals — with all those wonderful scenes of jealousy and passion that result. The Bertrams, and Rushworths, and Crawfords, and Fanny Price and Mrs. Norris would drive into Northampton, and go to the cinema. The wrong people might sit together, or Henry Crawford might press Fanny's hand in the dark: but there is little there for a novelist to get his teeth into.

§ 4 . THE REMOVAL OF OBSTACLES TO LOVE

There has been in this century such a relaxation of people's ideas about sexual morality, and, in particular, about marriage, that most people's emotional lives are very much freer and less complicated than they used to be. People may or may not be happier or better for this change — but for the novelist as such it is a change for the worse, for life is less interesting.

In *Sense and Sensibility* Edward Ferrars is unhappy through three-quarters of the book because, while he was under twenty-one, and not even legally bound by his promise, he had offered marriage to an underbred young woman, who has since appeared a worthless character to his more mature judgment. Life with Lucy must be unhappy; moreover Edward has now fallen in love seriously, and with a very superior woman in his own class, and has reason to believe that she is attached to him — but he may take no steps to break off his engagement.

Much later in the nineteenth century, it is thought dishonourable for the hero of *The Spoils of Poynton* not to fulfil his engagement to a most odious young woman, after he has come to dislike her as she deserves. He may not even play a waiting game, and hope that she will tire of him and give him up, though there is every chance of success in this line. He has to behave as if he were even impatient to marry her.

These two great novels must today be read with a 'willing suspension of disbelief' in the standards of honour maintained. Neither of these situations could occur today — or, if they did, the man would be thought so absurdly scrupulous that he would forfeit all sympathy.

It seems easier now, at any rate in fiction, to put an end to a marriage, than it was then to put an end to an engagement — and the social consequences are less disagreeable. It is therefore harder for a novelist to convince his readers by a picture of a desperately unhappy married life. Formerly husband or wife might cry: '*I can't get out!*' like Sterne's starling. That is not true any more: the door is open. Formerly there was no way out but Death, and that door could only be forced by Suicide or Murder — wonderful climaxes to a plot. A husband or wife who escapes by Suicide is now thought feeble; if either rids himself of a partner by Murder, it looks brutal and pointless.

There is a very good essay on this subject by Mr. Aldous Huxley, called *Obstacle Race*. He begins by a brief analysis of that strange novel by Stendhal, *Armance*, in which religion, convention, honour, delicacy and money one after another keep the lovers apart.

'Poor Octave!' says Mr. Huxley, 'Unhappy Armance! Their whole life was a kind of obstacle race — a climbing over and a crawling under barriers, a squeezing through narrow places. And the winning-post? For Octave the winning-post was a dose of laudanum; for Armance, a cell in a nunnery.

'If they had run their course today, they would have run it on the flat, or at any rate over a course irregular only by nature, not artificially obstructed. The going is easier now.'

Mr. Huxley went on to give as an example of flat-racing the love-stories of a Russian writer, whose sexual morality was merely that of the farmyard. Since the date of Mr. Huxley's essay, those who direct the destinies of Russia are said to have ordered many changes in these things — so much the better for the future of the Russian novel.

The most beautiful and skilful obstacle-racing in English fiction is probably to be found in *The Wings of the Dove*. The lovers' meeting in the park, at the beginning of this novel, is one of the most splendid in prose literature, simply because of the obstacles in their way. They themselves are fully aware of them, and Kate Croy almost glories in them — she is about to devise yet another obstacle, and one which will in the end, though she little knows it, keep them permanently apart. 'Yes,' she says, 'we're hideously intelligent. But there's fun in it too. We must get our fun where we can. I think our relation's beautiful. It isn't a bit *banal*. I cling to some saving romance in things.'

In too many recent novels the characters have only the most banal and unbeautiful relationships, and couple like animals, without the intelligence ever coming into play. There is no 'saving romance'.

Some French novelists have avoided the banality of flat-racing. Proust and Gide deal with sexual abnormality, which is still ringed round with complications; M. Mauriac deals with Catholics, who still recognize the existence of obstacles. Here are two fields for obstacle-racing indeed, but they have disadvantages. Those who write about Catholic or homosexual characters usually are consciously, rather too self-consciously, presenting them to a public which is neither homosexual nor Catholic, and from which a more or less 'willing suspension of disbelief' is therefore required: the difficulty of tone is quite exceptional. These are probably safer fields for French writers: a French novelist can without so much difficulty regard Catholic standards as a norm — and he is not awed by British criminal laws, or by British methods of banning books. It is sad to see these promising courses for obstacle-racing being levelled by some novelists into the dullest of flat race courses.

§ 5 . THE REMOVAL OF SOCIAL
OBSTACLES

Social life, as well as sexual life, is now very much less of an obstacle race than it used to be; most of the class-barriers are down. Our place in the social hierarchy is much less firmly fixed at birth. We are no longer confined by class in our choice of a profession. At one time Cabinet ministers were always gentlemen — today this is no longer the case. At one time gentlemen never became dentists — it is more than likely that there are now exceptions to this rule.

The lowering of barriers may, on the whole, be a good thing: but there is something to be said on the other side, and Burke has said it.

'I do not hesitate to say, that the road to eminence and power from obscure condition, ought not to be made too easy, nor a thing too much of course. If rare merit be the rarest of all things, it ought to pass through some sort of probation. The temple of honour ought to be seated on an eminence. If it be opened through virtue, let it be remembered too that virtue is never tried but by some difficulty and some struggle.'[2]

If this be applied to fiction, it is certainly true — for if the hero is to rise from obscure condition, it is the difficulties and struggles, precisely, that make the story. We are interested in the probation through which his virtue passes more than in his virtue itself — just as our interest in *Pamela* disappears when virtue is rewarded — and if it should happen to be the story of a failure and not a success, the experience conveyed may be no less significant.

It may be said that life today is freer and should be more interesting for people have more choice. The Brontës, daughters of a poor clergyman, had only two alternatives in life: to marry other clergymen, or to become governesses. Charlotte did both; her sisters died.

Today Charlotte Brontë might have edited a newspaper, might have sat in Parliament, might have toured the world on one or other of a hundred missions — she would probably have done some or all of these things. She would probably not have written so well.

A writer does not need wide experience so much as deep experience — and the wider experience is, the shallower it is likely to be. Even if there had still been that dramatic home at Haworth, and that drunken brother in the background — if Charlotte Brontë had been to a hundred other places, and had done a hundred other things as well as being a daughter at home — then that dramatic home at Haworth and that drunken brother would have sunk further into the background, would have mattered much less to her, and would not have been the same potent force of inspiration.

If Charlotte Brontë had been an important woman journalist, where would have been that pathetic dream of running a little school of her own with her sisters, which was only just impossible of realization, and was finally realized in that charming novel *Villette*?

§6. THE DEATH OF THE ORGANIC COMMUNITY

The organic community, which still exists as a permanent background to the novels of Jane Austen or Hardy, is no longer a living thing — and every modern novelist feels or exhibits its loss.

Jane Austen or Hardy looked out at country villages inhabited by labourers and landowners, by clergymen and doctors and their female dependents, by people who belonged there, and were functionally connected with the place. In Wessex there are already some strays: Lucetta at Casterbridge or Mrs. Charmond at Hintock, but they are not Hardy's more successful characters.

Today a number of houses may be inhabited by people whose real life and work is in the town, who live in the country only from Saturday to Monday, or who sleep there at night to be away from the noise, or merely because they cannot find room in the town. They may move house tomorrow — their tie to the place is feeble, and their relations with the other inhabitants are unreal and can be lightly broken.

If Jane Austen had been asked where she came from, she would at once have answered Hampshire — if Hardy had been asked, he would have answered Dorset — but many Englishmen, if asked what is their *pays*, do not know what to answer. Their parents have moved about, and so have they.

In consequence, their life has lacked depth and continuity. Many people in adult life know no one who was a child with them, no one who knew their parents. Social life is impoverished by restlessness and rootlessness — people do not live in one place for life, but are as transient as the English used to be in India, or as diplomats are *en poste* — life is therefore probably less interesting to live; it is certainly less interesting to write or to think about.

Jane Austen delighted to get her characters grouped in a village, where they were all fixed — at least for the time. If newcomers arrived, like the Dashwoods at Barton, the Crawfords at Mansfield, or Mr. Frank Churchill at Highbury, they came because they had connections with the place, and they were known and talked of before they appeared. Their visits were generally of some duration, and were likely to be repeated: they did not appear from nowhere, take a house furnished for three months, and then disappear without leaving a trace.

The modern novelist is often forced to resort to the most fluid and inorganic communities, that have been formed by no necessity, are kept together by no duties or loyalties, and will be broken up tomorrow — because he can find no more permanent group. A house-party in a country house used to be a popular subject — even that had the connection that all the guests must know at least their host or hostess, and some of them might antecedently know each other. There are fewer country house parties than there used to be, and novelists have gone on to show their people more loosely grouped in a hotel — or, worse, as travelling on the same train or ship.

There cannot in such circumstances be time or opportunity

for interesting relations to develop between them, or for any real, deep complication of motive.

The modern loneliness which results from the death of the organic community, in which nearly everyone had his place, is an interesting phenomenon — but it is the sort of phenomenon that is hard to exhibit in fiction, which gets its better effects from showing people together rather than in isolation. Nevertheless, like any other real experience, it is a possible theme for the novelist — and a better theme than contemporary social life often supplies. If we compare two novels of M. Sartre, we can see at a glance the great superiority of *La Nausée*, with its poignant picture of loneliness and isolation, to *L'Age de Raison*, where the people are indeed connected by personal relations of a sort, though these are of little strength or interest.

It may be said that nowadays it is easier to get about, and to meet a great number of people — and that this ought to help the novelist in his study of human nature. It is no compensation for the death of the organic community. There is much more to be learned from living in a constricted neighbourhood, and from seeing the same people again and again, year after year — in that way they force themselves on our attention. If we see too many people we cannot trouble to focus our eyes and minds upon them. Lazy focusing, which is said to be bad for the physical eyesight, is certainly bad for the mental vision.

Katherine Mansfield in her letters said that she wanted to know only a very few people: her husband, the friend she calls 'L. M.', a servant called Mrs. Honey. They helped her to people many of her best stories.

For the novel is a form of story-telling, and has a close affinity with a very humble intellectual activity, Gossip. You can only gossip effectively about people whom you know well, or people you know a great deal about. And gossip, and leisurely, gossippy letter-writing is the best breeding-ground for the novelist. It was the chat, and the chatty letters of a big family, that helped Jane Austen to develop into what she was: it was servant-girls' gossip that formed Samuel Richardson. Gossip is local, and it is not great travellers who have been the best letter-writers — it is people who have stayed at home, and have talked about their neighbours.

§7. WHAT REMAINS FOR THE NOVELIST

In the present age, man's inhumanity to man is less, if looked at from the private and social aspects, which alone interest the novelist; it is infinitely greater if looked at from a public or national aspect. Many obstacles are gone, and we can do a good deal of far and fast flat-racing; but we and our race course may be blown to bits by an atomic bomb. The atomic bomb may be devastating, but it is not at all interesting: it can only figure in one place in a plot — at the end. The obstacles, however, were really interesting, and might appear at any moment; moreover, they were a valuable stimulus to human ingenuity: there were all sorts of ways of dodging or of overcoming them. Our attitude to the atomic bomb can only be passive.

We must look for comfort where comfort is to be found. People are still human, and to be human is to err, and the world is not yet so mechanical that there is no room for human error. Individuals can (fortunately for the novelist) still do a great deal of harm, and cause a great deal of suffering — and though it is easier to escape from them than it used to be, there will always (or at least for a very long time) be people who cannot entirely escape from their neighbours' cruelty. And since it is individuals who feel the results of the misdeeds of the state, these misdeeds, though often not very interesting in themselves, may be interesting in their consequences — and from the cruelty of the state it is very much more difficult to escape than it used to be.

Moreover, although the human heart changes, it changes slowly. Most civilized people today would certainly say that Othello was a brutal fool — but though they would think it monstrous to murder Desdemona, however guilty she were, yet they would still think that, if Desdemona were guilty, Othello had the right to be very seriously annoyed. A dramatic critic who complained some years ago that the play was about nothing, was probably in the minority. However, a woman once told M. Mauriac that she could not understand *Phèdre*. 'What a lot of fuss about nothing!' she said. 'As if it wasn't the most natural thing in the world to fall in love with one's stepson!'[3]

People no doubt object to adultery very much less than they did — even a religious man might well, before he thought twice, be more angry if he were suspected of beating his own wife, than if he were suspected of seducing his neighbour's. Nevertheless people do object to it. If a time should come when no one objects — gone will be a favourite subject for the novelist. Even so, moral standards could, for a limited time, survive in fiction their extinction elsewhere — just as some ideals of honour have lingered on in drama after they were dead in everyday life.[4] Even in a Huxleyan brave new world a novelist might be able to write historical novels about ages in which the human race had still been human — if he and his readers retained sufficient semblance of humanity.

And even now, if we feel over much grieved at the collapse of obstacles, at the tediousness of most people's working-life, at the death of the organic community, it is in our power to

27

revive all these things by placing the action of our novels a few years back into the past. This is what Miss Compton-Burnett has done. She is thus enabled to depict a world unshaken by modern warfare, a community rooted in a single place, and lives still ruled, and even laid waste, by family tyranny. She can do this, because she need only take a period fifty years ago, when she was herself already alive — therefore she can recreate this age without the artificiality and falsity of the historical novelist. Younger writers can hardly do the same thing, and she is, too probably, the last person who can do it successfully. Already this device causes some readers to make the mistake of dismissing her novels as 'Quaint' — but in time their date of publication may cease to be relevant, and they may come to seem novels of English life between 1888 and 1910, which might have been written at any time. It is to be hoped that this will be the case; it would be a sad thing if a novelist whose powers are little, if at all, inferior to Jane Austen's, should be forced, owing to the unpropitious age in which she lives, to occupy no higher place in the history of the novel than that of, say, Peacock. There is reason to hope for the happier alternative: contemporaneity is not very important to the novelist, and Jane Austen, Scott, Dickens, Thackeray and George Eliot did their best work with no regard to it.

This for our wisest . . .

We others have still nooks and crannies of life to pry into, and oddities to bring to light. The modern novelist might say, with one of Miss Compton-Burnett's characters: 'It is little, unnatural corners of the world that appeal to me. I am very overcivilized.' Good minor work may be raised on these little, unnatural corners — and given a fortunate combination of the man, the experience, and the 'objective correlative', good major work is by no means impossible. Balzac built some of his best work on just such little, unnatural corners of the world — it should still be possible to write such a book as *Le Curé de Tours*, and who has the right to wish to write anything better?

Of little, unnatural corners of the human mind, more is known; psychology may help us to investigate some of them. And though we lose infinitely much by the relaxation of tabus about what people may do, we may gain a little by the relaxation of a few tabus about what people may say. Subjects hitherto denied to us may no longer be withheld. Thackeray complained that no novelist since Fielding had been permitted' to exhibit the whole man; now we have all Fielding's freedom and more. Thackeray would have liked to give Arthur Pendennis something of the sex-life of Tom Jones; but Fielding had been reticent about some aspects of Tom Jones's life — he did not, for example, explore his digestion as James Joyce has explored that of Bloom. Yet we have not, perhaps, gained so very much in gaining the freedom of the character's alimentary canal: it can tell us a great deal about the character, but things that might have been learned more interestingly from his words and behaviour — and even admiring readers of Lawrence must confess to boredom with the physical details of his people's loves.

Nevertheless, though the prospect is not very cheerful, there are probably as many subjects left in life as ever came out of it. It is not yet time to despair of the novel, or to decide that nothing but a serious operation can give it renewed life.

§ 8. THE MYTH OF THE DAUGHTERS
OF PELIAS

The sorceress Medea cut an old ram into pieces, boiled them in a caldron of water with a few herbs, and out jumped a fine young lamb. She persuaded the daughters of Pelias to try a similar experiment upon their father, in order to rejuvenate him. It was a trick, and they found they had only made him into soup.

So, when we are invited to admire the 'broken time-scheme' or some other experiment, whether of Mr. Aldous Huxley, or Mr. Philip Toynbee, or anyone else — it is proper to inquire: Has the novel sprung with renewed life from their caldrons, or have they merely made soup of its poor old bones?

NOTES

[1] *The Letters of Katherine Mansfield*, ed. J. Middleton Murry, I, p. 278: November 10th, 1919.

[2] *Reflections on the Revolution in France.*

[3] *Le Roman*, p. 14.

[4] The standards of honour maintained in *The Spoils of Poynton* are no doubt already a survival.

II

FOUR RELATED QUESTIONS

§ I. THE FOUR QUESTIONS

There are four questions of some importance in the criticism of fiction which are too seldom asked. No final answer to these questions can be expected, but this does not mean that it is merely idle curiosity to ask them: every time they are honestly raised, some small contribution towards solving them is likely to be made.

I. Can a good novel be a poor work of art?

And the converse:

II. Can a good work of art, which is in the form of a novel, be a poor novel (or poor as a novel)?

And two related questions:

III. Is it possible to say something significant, and yet write bad prose?

IV. Can prose be good when its content is insignificant?

Many people would answer all these questions unhesitatingly in the negative, and it is true that almost all the critical preconceptions that we have acquired in the second quarter of this century incline us to such an answer.

We have learned to repudiate the vicious distinction between 'style' and 'subject-matter', and the admiration for 'beautiful English', in which many of us were brought up by old-fashioned school-masters. In all branches of literature we have been shown the inseparability of the thing said from the way we say it — and of course philosophers have always known, even if men of letters have sometimes forgotten, that a thing said in

31

two different ways is never precisely the same thing said, and that if we say a thing beyond a point badly, we have failed to say it. Mr. I. A. Richards in *Practical Criticism*, and other critics who have adopted his methods, have taught us to look very closely at the texture both of prose and verse, and few will dissent from Mrs. Leavis when she writes: 'the essential technique in an art that works by using words is the way in which words are used'.[1]

Moreover Mr. T. S. Eliot has maintained against William Archer that a play cannot be a good play and yet be bad literature, and that in poetic drama poetry and drama are the same thing[2] — he has even given us the impression that the better the poetry is the better the drama will be[3] (though, if he ever held this view, he must have revised it before writing *The Cocktail Party*). We are likely to reason for ourselves that a novel cannot be a good novel and yet be bad literature, and that in prose fiction the prose and the fiction are the same thing — we may even go further and opine that the better the prose is, the better the fiction must be (or vice versa).

§ 2. WHETHER DISTINCTIVE NAMES FOR DIFFERENT LITERARY GENRES ARE OF USE

It may first be pertinently inquired if there is any value at all in the traditional names for the different literary genres: drama, the novel, the essay, biography, etc. Should we confine ourselves to some general term, such as 'Literature', for the art that works by using words; and is it not enough in each work that comes under our notice, to examine the way in which words are used? Even such broad distinctions as Poetry and Prose might be done away with, since no two people are in agreement about them any more than they are over the meaning of the word 'gentleman'. Moreover the existence of 'Free Verse' has blunted the more easily drawn distinction between Verse and Prose: for who will presume to say how free Verse can be, and yet remain, Verse?

The traditional names for the genres are often misleading in literary history: we find 'histories of the novel', for instance, which neglect the influence of Dryden on Richardson, because Dryden was not one of his 'precursors in the novel'. While in many important activities of criticism, such as the assignment of merit, these names have often no help to give.

This speech of Mrs. Gamp's, for instance, may be called prose or verse.

Which, Mr. Chuzzlewit, is well beknown to Mrs. Harris
As has one sweet infant (though she *do* not wish it known)
In her own family by the mother's side,
Kep' in spirits in a bottle;
And that sweet babe she see at Greenwich Fair,
A travelling in company with the pink-eyed lady, Prooshan
    dwarf, and living skelinton,
Which judge her feelin's when the barrel-organ played,
And she was showed her own dear sister's child,
The same not bein' expected from the outside picter,
Where it was painted quite contrairy in a livin' state,
A many sizes larger,
And performing beautiful upon the Arp,
Which never did that dear child know or do:
Since breathe it never did, to speak on, in this wale!
And Mrs. Harris, Mr. Chuzzlewit,
Has knowed me many a year, and can give you information
That the lady which is widdered can't do better

And may do worse than let me wait upon her,
Which I hope to do.
Permittin' the sweet faces as I see afore me.

If this is prose, with the eighteenth-century novelists to set the standard, or subtle, dramatic verse, in which Jacobean comedy lives again, it hardly matters — it is magnificent, whether verse or prose. While the death of little Nell is contemptible writing, whether it be regarded as prose or verse.

Unlike the productions of the plastic arts, we can never say of a literary work that its creator mistook his medium — as when a sculptor makes out of bronze a statue that would have been more appropriate in porcelain. The literary artist has only one medium: words. Nor, as in Music, can we ever say that a literary work has been wrongly scored, for there is only one instrument that could ever perform it, the human voice — and whether soprano or baritone, spoken aloud or in the head, makes no difference at all.

Literary works cannot be differentiated by the medium in which they are executed, or by the instruments for which they have been written. Can they, like architectural monuments, be differentiated by the purpose for which they are made?

Function is less valuable an artistic criterion than it has sometimes been thought. 'The first qualification for judging any piece of workmanship from a corkscrew to a cathedral is to know *what* it is,' writes Mr. C. S. Lewis, '—what it was intended to do and how it is meant to be used ... as long as you think the corkscrew was meant for opening tins or the cathedral for entertaining tourists you can say nothing to the purpose about them.'[4] This sounds disarmingly reasonable, and indeed the general form of corkscrew or cathedral is determined by its function — the necessity to get a good grip on a cork or (among other things) to provide a sizable choir and a number of altars for the use of a college of canons. But these functions can be served equally well by beautiful or ugly corkscrews or cathedrals. And a significant work of art can often, in later times, be put to purposes for which its creator never intended it. The builders of Salisbury cathedral were equally far from supposing that it would ever be used for the choral offices of the Church of England, for organ recitals of eighteenth-century music, or for the entertainment of American tourists — for all of which purposes it is exquisitely well adapted. And so long as any literary work continues to delight (whether or no it was once also meant to instruct) we cannot call it a failure.[5]

The analogy of Architecture does suggest that while we can certainly say of a theatre, for example, that it is a pretty building, but an inefficient theatre — or that it is an admirable theatre, but a hideous building, it may not be absolutely impossible to make some sort of parallel distinction in Literature. But any parallel between the arts is misleading if drawn too far — works of Literature have a more obvious duty to delight and a less obvious duty to be useful than most works of Architecture, and works of Architecture fall more disastrously to the ground if they are ill constructed.

§ 3. THE INCONVENIENCE OF REJECTING THESE NAMES

If we repudiate the traditional names for the literary genres, and refuse to speak of the drama, the novel, etc., then our first two questions disappear. We have only to ask of a literary work if it is, or is not, a good work of art. But as long as we retain these names, then these questions are at least not meaningless,

C   S.P.F.   35

and can certainly be asked, even if they should turn out to be no more than questions about the meaning of words.

But it does not seem so easy to get rid of all these names. Some could indeed go without much loss: the ode has long been divorced from any idea of a public, ceremonial performance, and lyric poetry has nothing more to do with the lyre. But drama has not yet lost all suggestion of an action performed before an audience seated in a theatre — and good art which would not please an intelligent and sensitive audience under those conditions may reasonably be called 'undramatic'. And Mr. Eliot finds himself forced to admit a distinction between dramatic and purely poetic values when he writes: 'Heywood's versification is never on a very high poetic level, but at its best is often on a high dramatic level.'[6]

It is unlikely that drama is the only name that must be retained: it looks as if each name should be retained or rejected on its own merits. And perhaps it is a convenience to have a name for prose fictions, for the narrative representation of character in action.

Though we do not, before the event, have to have names for the things we are going to do, yet we generally have to find names for the things we are going to make. A sinner, for example, will probably not say to himself: 'I am now going to commit fornication; I shall now perpetrate calumny,' or the like. But a writer does not sit down to make a literary work any more than a cook stands up to make a work of culinary art — the writer proposes to make, say, a novel, and the cook a soufflé.

Moreover no good writer ever directly aims at self-expression, or the criticism of life, when engaged in creative work — he wants to make a definite work, through which he may indeed be found to have expressed himself, and to have commented on the world around him. And if the work he has tried to make involves the representation of characters in action, then the critic may properly inquire how he has represented characters in action, and not only how he has used words. It is certain that a man may use words very well indeed, and yet be quite incapable of representing characters in action: it is not quite so certain that a man can use words clumsily or ill, and yet succeed in this — but it may be so.

§4. THE CHILD-MIND IN FICTION

It may be so; and, if it is so, then a form of criticism entirely directed towards 'the way in which words are used' will come to grief. It may be so, because the creative artist in Literature is not always a person of the highest intelligence — any more than the creative artist in the other arts. His mind is imaginative rather than philosophical — like Rickie Elliot in Mr. Forster's novel *The Longest Journey* (himself a creative writer), he fills imaginary pastures with imaginary cows, plashing knee-deep by the brink of impassable rivers, while the abstract mind is inquiring whether external objects exist when they are not seen. Lower parts of the mind are the novelist's province — memory, for example, which is sometimes despised by the abstract thinker as merely mechanical, and rather bad mechanism at that. ''Tis better to own a Judgment,' wrote Glanvill, 'Tho' but with a *curta supellex* of coherent notions; then a *memory*, like a Sepulchre, furnished with a load of broken and discarnate bones.' But the novelist does not require so very much judgment — he waits for breath to come from the four winds and breathe upon the dry bones, that they may rise again, but combined in a new way, and so his fiction is born.

The novelist's sensibility may be greater than his intelligence, but even this is limited — the highest sensibility is more likely to appreciate than to create. Some very primitive factors are involved in creation — in particular, cruelty. Drama is more akin to mimicry, the novel to gossip and even scandal-mongering, than either of them are to Science or Philosophy — and the primitive factors in Literature cannot be neglected or despised, they are the forces that make it live. (This does not mean that a novelist should not educate such intelligence and sensibility as he possesses as well as he can.)

A child, or an otherwise immature mind, can be observant and also creative about human beings and the relations between them — can even be extremely subtle and penetrating about more highly evolved beings than itself, even if it is in the dark about many of their interests. 'What a creator of character needs', says Mr. Eliot, 'is not so much knowledge of motives as keen sensibility; the dramatist need not understand people; but he must be exceptionally aware of them.'⁷ For this reason the advance of psychology has done very much less for fiction than people, not novelists, expected it would: it can help us to understand people, but it cannot increase our awareness of them.

Henry James's Maisie did not even know what are so often and so oddly called 'the facts of life' — and yet she anxiously and shrewdly followed the couplings and uncouplings of her immoral parents and step-parents, with a sensitive awareness of which the Queen's Proctor is unlikely to have been capable.

Any intelligent book about an intelligent child is likely to make the same point. 'I could observe', says David Copperfield of his youthful self, 'in little pieces, as it were; but as to making a net of a number of these pieces, and catching anybody in it, that was, as yet, beyond me!' Nevertheless we see the pieces beginning to cohere — and they are always sharply observed.

It is not only sentimentality to say that 'children always know', and perhaps the same proposition about animals is less ridiculous than it is often thought. If we know what we mean, then we may say that (some) children and animals 'know': for this reason it is much more humiliating to be rebuffed when we court the friendship of these creatures, than to find ourselves getting on badly with a journalist, for example, or a society woman whom we have met for the first time.

§5. THE CASE OF CHARLOTTE YONGE

Charlotte Yonge, who is as probably in heaven as any novelist, if not a little child, was not much more grown up than a pious schoolgirl, whose favourite treat is a missionary meeting. We cannot call hers an interesting mind, no abstract speculations of hers could hold us for a moment, and it is unlikely that she would ever influence us in matters of taste. But in practical matters she knew the difference between Right and Wrong, and she was unusually observant and sensitive about people and the relations between them. If she and Galsworthy, to name no living novelist, were both present at some occasion of human interest, it is surely to her that one would go for an eye-witness account, or from her that one would prefer to receive a letter about it — just as there are school-children with whom one would rather gossip than with first-rate literary critics.

Therefore her biographers may well speak of her 'ageless books, marked by an understanding of the constant elements in human nature',[8] and it will often be found that other novelists enjoy reading them — they are uninteresting only to those who are not interested in people.

It is instructive to compare her famous novel, *The Heir of Redclyffe*, with *Amabel and Mary Verena*, a sequel by Mrs. Hicks

Beach. The earlier writer was incomparably the more creative: she has given a splendid vitality and idiosyncracy to her characters, otherwise Mrs. Hicks Beach would not have wished to write more of them, and would not have found any readers if she had. The characters of *The Heir of Redclyffe* live, but live in our minds like people we ourselves knew in adolescence (if we were very observant), or like people who have been described to us by observant but simple gossips. And, after all, the simple narrator has often been chosen by novelists, and has been a successful literary device: we owe much of our knowledge of the happenings at Wuthering Heights and at Thrushcross Grange to Nelly Dean, and Esther Summerson has kept us similarly informed about the happenings at Bleak House. One advantage in the simple narrator is that the reader feels that he does not know all, and therefore the characters have the mysterious vitality of living people: we can therefore take sides about the fictitious characters, as we can about people in real life, and in history — it is possible to read *Wuthering Heights* from a pro-Heathcliff, or a pro-Linton point of view, accepting either the romantic values of Wuthering Heights (by a willing suspension of disbelief) or the values of Thrushcross Grange, which are those of any sane morality. Similarly, in *The Heir of Redclyffe*, Guy and Amy may be our hero and heroine, or Philip and Laura.

There is, however, a great difference between the simple narrator, and the simple author. Nelly Dean and Esther Summerson are controlled by the higher intelligence of their creators, and therefore *Wuthering Heights* and *Bleak House* are significant works of art — a term which one cannot apply to a work in which no more developed mind than that of Charlotte Yonge is in evidence.

The sequel to *The Heir of Redclyffe*, by Mrs. Hicks Beach, is a most interesting commentary. A less creative but far more intelligent writer has understood Charlotte Yonge's characters more profoundly than she could have done herself, for much of their lives lay outside her range. Charlotte Yonge could never have 'gone behind' Charles, nor could she have revealed Philip's limitations; he was at any rate cleverer and better educated than she was, and had gained over her much the same ascendancy as he enjoyed over most of the women in the book. When reading *Amabel and Mary Verena*, we feel that we are re-visiting in maturity people whom we have intimately known but imperfectly understood in early life — they seem smaller perhaps, even as places are said to shrink when revisited.

It is hard to avoid the conviction that Charlotte Yonge has presented character with some success, and that in a limited, but not negligible, sense *The Heir of Redclyffe* is a good novel, though not a significant work of art.

§6. THE GOOD BOOK WHICH IS A BAD NOVEL

If, however, we have to maintain that a significant work of art, which happens to be a novel, must be a good novel, then we are not far from the position of Miss Jenkyns in *Cranford* — we have no argument to oppose to her.

She had unwillingly been obliged to listen to poor Captain Brown reading the account of the 'swarry' which Sam Weller gave at Bath.

'When it was ended, she turned to me, and said with mild dignity — "Fetch me 'Rasselas', my dear, out of the book-room."

'When I had brought it to her, she turned to Captain Brown —

'"Now allow *me* to read you a scene, and then the present company can judge between your favourite, Mr. Boz, and Dr. Johnson."

'She read one of the conversations between Rasselas and Imlac, in a high-pitched, majestic voice: and when she had ended, she said, "I imagine I am now justified in my preference of Dr. Johnson as a writer of fiction." '

It is pleasant to reflect that Dr. Johnson would not probably have shared this preference. Though his remarks about Fielding are hostile, he could not have been insensitive to the quality of his writing; and though he may have felt Richardson's vulgarities less than Lady Mary Wortley Montagu did, they are likely to have struck him more forcibly than they strike most readers today — and yet he could declare: 'Sir, there is more knowledge of the heart in one letter of Richardson's, than in all *Tom Jones*.'

And yet *Rasselas* hardly succeeds as a novel — if, indeed, it was ever intended to do so — though worthy of all Miss Jenkyns's admiration as a book. As it is a book couched in the form of a novel, with characters and actions, then it would probably be an even better book if we could take any interest in those characters and actions — if, for example, the misfortunes of Pekuah had any power to move us. It is only through its brevity that it remains readable, and escapes that 'violent tediousness' which even such an admirer of D. H. Lawrence as Richard Aldington finds in his novels.

It is often objected, and with reason, that criticism which speaks of Form and Content, Plot and Character, Colour and Design, and the like is vicious — for it is putting asunder what God has joined; it is an artificial separation of what is, in each case, a single process, for the sake of a fruitless analysis. But only too often the single process, which is characteristic of the satisfactory work of art, has not taken place — the fatal split between two parts of what should have been a single process can only too often be discerned. It is when Form and Content, Plot and Character, etc., are straining apart, or are in some way incompatible, that it is still worth talking about them.

§7. BAD PROSE WITH A SIGNIFICANT CONTENT: HARDY

We may proceed to the second two questions, even more fundamental, about the separation of prose from its subject matter.

A passage from Hardy provides a convenient object-lesson.

'To persons standing alone on a hill during a clear midnight such as this, the roll of the world eastward is almost a palpable movement. The sensation may be caused by the panoramic glide of the stars past earthly objects, which is perceptible in a few minutes of stillness, or by the better outlook upon space that a hill affords, or by the wind, or by the solitude; but whatever be its origin, the impression of riding along is vivid and abiding. The poetry of motion is a phrase much in use, and to enjoy the epic form of that gratification it is necessary to stand on a hill at a small hour of the night, and, having first expanded with a sense of difference from the rest of civilized mankind, who are dreamwrapt and disregardful of all such proceedings at this time, long and quietly to watch your stately progress through the stars. After such a nocturnal reconnoitre it is hard to get back to earth, and to believe that the consciousness of such majestic speeding is derived from a tiny human frame.'

Lord David Cecil has chosen this passage from *Far From the Madding Crowd* for especial praise. 'Its detail', he writes of Hardy's vision of the natural world here expressed, 'endows it with the concrete recognizable actuality of something we know. It has also the compelling imaginative power of a picture which exhibits something known in a new, grander perspective, extending our field of vision so that we see what we know in relation to the greater conditioning forces we do not know. Incidentally, the passage is an illustration of how a strong creative imagination can make use of what might seem the most intractable material. The scientific view of the universe, introduced in the Victorian age, is a grim affair. Hardy was only too well aware of this . . . But the poet in him was undefeatable, and revealed through his eyes, it becomes the opportunity for a new sort of poetry — an awe-inspiring vision of infinite spaces and mysterious, irresistible forces — as compelling to the fancy as any primitive belief in the gods of wind and earth and fire.'[9]

This passage has a grand and cosmic beauty, one is ready to agree, and yet Mr. Denys Thompson has picked it out for especial condemnation. 'Strained, lumbering, creaking with polysyllables because the author thinks them "literary" ',[10] is his comment — and this also is true.

How horrible some of the phrases are! 'A palpable movement . . . The poetry of motion is a phrase much in use . . . to enjoy the epic form of that gratification . . . disregardful of all such proceedings . . . nocturnal reconnoitre.' Not to mince words, this is ugly, bad writing — and many persons of taste could easily rewrite such a passage to its great improvement — though they could never have seized the original feeling that inspired it, to which Lord David Cecil has done justice. This is another proof, if proof were required, that we need both 'academic' and 'practical' criticism — critics who see the wood, as well as critics who see the trees.

Hardy has said what he has to say very badly, but not so

badly that he has failed to say it: his meaning is significant, and can be apprehended as significant, though expressed in very bad prose. And if some of the blemishes were removed from this passage, the slight changes that we should make in the meaning (for a change of word is a change of meaning — and we have learned that there are no synonyms) would actually improve the meaning. For example, if we were to begin the third sentence thus: 'To enjoy the poetry of motion in its epic form'; if we were to omit the weak and clumsy phrase 'disregardful of all such proceedings', and to substitute such a word as 'adventure', or 'experience' for 'nocturnal reconnoitre' — the meaning on the whole would be clearer and sharper, and nothing that mattered would have been lost.

A significant meaning has to be apprehended through the ugly texture of the prose in the work of other mature writers — very often in that of George Eliot. And good writers, not yet mature, often know what they want to say, before they know how to say it — for example, it is sometimes difficult to make out how sensitively a complicated situation has been handled by L. H. Myers in *The Orissers*, because the book is not well enough written.

§8. EUPHONY

It must not, however, be thought that by some divine system of pre-established harmony the best meaning is always expressible in the best words, and that the prose-writer has only to be quite clear in his mind about what he wants to say. Euphony has also to be considered — and Flaubert's patient toil, removing repetitions, and assonances, and double genitives, was not a waste of time. The simplest and most lucid expression of a meaning may well be ungainly.[11]

It is sometimes best to write ungainly prose. A philosopher who wishes to express very fine shades of meaning, and whose aim is at all costs to be understood, and not at all to give pleasure, is justified in making a total sacrifice of euphony. Moreover, the use of precise, but ugly, philosophical jargon sometimes prevents the philosopher, as well as his readers, from getting into a muddle — Locke wrote euphonious English, and in consequence we do not always know, and it seems that he was not always sure, what precise meaning he attached to the word 'idea'.

The creative artist, novelist as well as poet, seldom has such a fine point of sense to convey as the philosopher — but his task in the use of words is no easier — he has often to convey a fine point of feeling. And here ugly but precise psychological jargon is no help to him at all, but quite the contrary. His art is that of rhetoric rather than dialectic — without some degree of euphony, and without great sensitiveness in the choice of words, he cannot make the reader feel the feeling that he wishes to convey. For we apprehend Sense no matter how ugly its expression is, so long as it is lucid and grammatical: from this point of view, the notices of births and deaths in the newspapers are perfectly adequate. It is when the advertisers have the bad taste to advertise also their feelings about these events that we are embarrassed — for feelings cannot be conveyed without art, though facts can.

§9. STYLE AND MEANING

We can perhaps return to the position that Style is not separable from Meaning, if by Meaning we understand the total Meaning — which Mr. I. A. Richards has analysed into four parts: Sense, Feeling, Tone and Intention — Feeling being the writer's attitude to the Sense he wishes to communicate; Tone, his attitude towards the readers with whom he wishes to communicate; and Intention the aims which he wishes to promote.[12]

With this for our definition of Meaning, we can endorse Flaubert's teaching, as reported by Maupassant: 'whatever the thing is that one wishes to say, there is only one word to express it, one verb to animate it, and one adjective to qualify it. Therefore one must search until one has found them, this word, this verb, this adjective.'[13]

The writer has to struggle with the claims of Sense, Tone, Feeling and Intention, which may not always be pulling the same way, and finally he has to wrestle with the angel of his language, and he must not let it go until it has blessed him — and Euphony is one of the blessings in its gift.

It is natural that many writers have seen all writing as translation. 'The duty and task of a writer', says Proust, 'are those of a translator.'[14] And Conrad writes: 'To render a crucial point of feelings in terms of human speech is really an impossible task. Written words can only form a sort of translation. And if that translation happens, from want of skill or from over-anxiety, to be too literal, the people caught in the toils of passion, instead of disclosing themselves, which would be art, are made to give themselves away, which is neither art nor life.'[15]

Poetry may sometimes be the 'original', but Prose is almost always 'translation' — and while Poetry, even when it is not great Poetry, has often reached its final state, Prose, as Katherine Mansfield discovered, 'is never finished'.

§ 10. CAN PROSE BE GOOD WHEN ITS CONTENT IS INSIGNIFICANT?

We are now in a better position not to answer the fourth question, for such questions cannot be answered, but to discover lines along which an answer may be sought.

Even when we know better, we are still prone to identify Meaning with its first part, Sense. If we give Meaning this limited meaning, then Form and Content are very much more easily separable: all that belongs to Feeling, Tone and Intention will be reckoned as part of the Form. It will then be easy to find very good prose which has no significant content. Letters, for example, by Cowper, and other excellent letter-writers, are often ostensibly about nothing — but while the Sense they convey is negligible, they are exquisite little masterpieces of Tone and Feeling.

We have been taught, by ancient works on Rhetoric, to recognize the merit of writing in which Intention is the prime element — when the orator wishes to urge his hearers to action, to resist Philip or to condemn Verres. We still lack a Rhetoric of Tone and Feeling.

But before we rise to the study of Rhetoric, there is the humble, essential and too much neglected study of Grammar to be made. 'Beautiful English' is an unfortunate conception, and unhappy are those who try to write it; 'Dignified English' is a language into which the Greek and Latin classics are too often translated — it is much the same thing as the jargon described by Fowler as 'Wardour Street'; but there is such a thing as 'Good English' — and it is Grammar that tells us what it is, and it can be learned and taught.

§ II. GRAMMAR MAY BE ABSENT FROM GOOD PROSE

We can and should admire such a speech as Mrs. Gamp's, in which Grammar (the wider term also includes Syntax) is set at naught. Its relation to a beautiful speech by an illiterate person in real life is much the same as the relation we discussed between the narrative of a simple narrator directed by a great artist (Nelly Dean or Esther Summerson) and the narrative of a naturally simple narrator (Charlotte Yonge).

Mr. Herbert Read is right in asking us to admire Vanzetti's great speech to Judge Thayer. 'If it had not been for these thing, I might have live out my life, talking at street corners to scorning men. I might have die, unmarked, unknown, a failure. Now we are not a failure. This is our career and our triumph. Never in our full life can we hope to do such work for tolerance, for joostice, for man's understanding of man, as now we do by an accident. Our words — our lives — our pains — nothing! The taking of our lives — lives of a good shoemaker and a poor fish peddler — all! That last moment belong to us — that agony is our triumph!'[16]

Mr. Read is right in saying that though this speech is devoid of all 'artistry' and of all deliberate structure, it has the elements of great prose. It would be barren pedantry to deny that this great tragic speech had the elements of great prose; it would be sentimentality to say that it was great prose. But the great comic speech of Mrs. Gamp has a very great artist behind it, moulding its deliberate structure — it is great prose. A great artist in prose must know his grammar, even if he chooses to play tricks with it.

If we take Meaning to be the total meaning: Sense, Feeling, Tone and Intention — and if Style is the Expression of that Meaning, and inseparable from it — then we can give new life to the old cliché *le style est l'homme*, for we are what we mean.

We are not the same at all times, and we probably ought to take care to purify ourselves from our worst passions before writing — or at any rate we ought not to write for the public when we are at our worst, any more than we should write private letters in a temper.

'A certain transfusion takes place upon paper', wrote the Abbé de St. Cyran, 'of the spirit and heart of the writer, and is the cause of one perceiving, so to speak, his image in the picture of the thing which he represents . . . The smallest cloud in our heart will spread on our paper, like a bad breath that tarnishes the whole surface of a mirror, and our smallest indisposition will be like a worm that passes into our writing, to gnaw the heart of those who read it to the end of the world.'[17]

This is, of course, exaggerated scrupulosity — and if a novelist were to accept Jansenist direction, he must throw down his pen; we know well enough the words of Pierre Nicole: 'A writer of novels and a dramatic poet is a public poisoner, not of bodies but of the souls of the faithful, and should regard himself as guilty of an infinite number of spiritual homicides.'[18]

It is in the spirit of Nicole that the English laws about obscenity have been framed, and most enlightened people think them rather a pity. We are not responsible for the effects of our writing on other people further than our intention goes — Benjamin Constant was wrong in being shocked when Goethe told him that he did not care if *Werther* were dangerous reading for fools, for Goethe was not writing for fools. But for our intention we are totally and gravely responsible, and it is a most serious duty to keep it pure. It would be better if contemporary criticism were more exacting about authors' purity of intention, and troubled less about their idealogies. And purity of intention is to be deduced by the methods of literary criticism, and no others, from style not biography — for a vicious man can sometimes remain a virtuous writer.[1]

All the same, a writer had better be as good as he can be, were it only for the sake of his writing. Fowler, in *Modern English Usage*, has clearly shown that many faults in writing spring from real faults in feeling and character; they are not only due to bad taste and to literary ill-breeding, but to moral faults, such as envy, hypocrisy, vanity and cowardice. If the style is the man, the man has always room for improvement.[2]

And conversely, the man may be improved by the improvement of the style; for improvement can proceed both from the heart outwards, and from without inwards to the heart. The thought need not surprise us: anyone who has heard sermons is familiar with the duty of controlling that unruly member the tongue — and everything that we have been told about the tongue is equally true about our eleventh finger, the pen, except that the pen is much easier to control. If we could as easily go back and erase or emend our speeches, our lives would be happier: our writing need never be hurried, ill-considered, or ill-tempered.

If, with Fowler for our director, we were to rid our style of vanity, envy, hypocrisy and cowardice, we should have gone a long way towards being more courageous and more truthful.

NOTES

[1] *Fiction and the Reading Public*, p. 232f.
[2] *Selected Essays*, pp. 110ff.
[3] Ibid., pp. 50ff.

[4] *A Preface to Paradise Lost*, p. 1.

[5] What are we to say of such works as the novels of Amanda Ros, which are supposed to give delight because they are so bad? The authoress certainly did not intend them to give the kind of delight that they give, but they cannot be said to be a failure. It is surely some strange kind of excellence that gives delight, not badness, which is merely dull.

[6] Loc. cit., p. 175.

[7] Ibid., p. 132, and see chap. v, s.v. 'Knowledge of Motives'.

[8] *Victorian Best-seller: the world of Charlotte M. Yonge*, by MARGARET MARE and ALICIA PERCIVAL, p. 5.

[9] *Hardy the Novelist*, p. 73.

[10] *Reading and Discrimination*, ad fin. Cf. the criticisms of Hardy in GEORGE MOORE's *Conversations in Ebury Street*.

[11] For a discussion of Euphony, see *The Summing-Up*, by W. SOMERSET MAUGHAM.

[12] *Practical Criticism*, pp. 179ff.

[13] *Le Roman* (preface to *Pierre et Jean*).

[14] *Le Temps Retrouvé*, II, p. 41.

[15] Preface to *Within the Tides*.

[16] *English Prose Style*, p. 165.

[17] Cit. SAINTE BEUVE, *Port Royal*, II, ix.

[18] Ibid., VI, x. Cf. 'Nous savons d'expérience que le même ouvrage qui aide au salut de beaucoup d'âmes en peut corrompre plusieurs autres. Cela est vrai, même de l'Ecriture.' FRANÇOIS MAURIAC, *La Roman*, p. 78.

[19] Cf. *A Treatise on the Novel*, p. 60 and note.

[20] It has been pointed out to me, however, by M. Cyril des Baux, that the Devil should be given his due: he has inspired some works of art. He adds that certain works of Gide owe their quality to hypocrisy.

III

SUMMARY

§ I. SUMMARY

All narrative art is made up of Summary and Scene: if there were no Summary it would be dramatic and not narrative, and if there were no Scene, as we shall see, it would not be art.

Even Drama itself finds difficulty in getting on without Summary. When it is read, and not seen on the stage, some form of stage directions are necessary — whether they are the brief indications of the speakers' names which sufficed in the great ages of Drama, or the long descriptive passages to which we have become accustomed in the decadence of that art in the hands of Barrie and Shaw.

Even in great ages of Drama it was necessary to put stage directions from time to time into the mouths of characters — to disguise, in fact, this form of Summary as Scene.

Examples leap to the mind:

> *There stands the castle by yon tuft of trees . . .*

or the lines in *Bérénice*, that so much amused Horace Walpole:

> *De son appartement cette porte est prochaine,*
> *Et cette autre conduit dans celuy de la Reine.*

Stage representation can nowadays replace that sort of thing in most cases, but it can do nothing to obviate the tiresome process, necessarily narrative and non-dramatic, which Henry James called 'Harking back to make up'.[1]

This process has been admirably parodied by Sheridan:[2]

SIR WALTER   You know, my friend, scarce two revolving suns
              And three revolving moons have closed their
                course,
              Since haughty Philip, in despite of peace,
              With hostile hand hath struck at England's
                trade.

SIR CHRISTOPHER   I know it well.

SIR WALTER   Philip, you know, is proud Iberia's king!

SIR CHRISTOPHER   He is.

SIR WALTER   His subjects in base bigotry
              And Catholic oppression held, — while we
              You know, the Protestant persuasion hold.

SIR CHRISTOPHER   We do.

Dangle. Mr. Puff, as he *knows* all this, why does Sir Walter go on telling him?

Puff. But the audience are not supposed to know anything of the matter, are they?

Sneer. True, but I think you manage ill: for there certainly appears no reason why Sir Walter should be so communicative.

Puff. 'Fore Gad, now, that is one of the most ungrateful observations I ever heard — for the less inducement he has to tell this the more, I think, you ought to be obliged to him; for I am sure you'd know nothing of the matter without it.

The cinema can flash upon the screen a printed summary of any information needed by the audience. Elizabethan drama could tell us things in the soliloquy (though First and Second Gentlemen or Citizens did a good deal of 'harking back to make up'). And in Greek drama the Gods themselves could appear in the prologue to supply necessary information. It is only in a realistic play on a modern picture-stage that this process is merely absurd. It requires a good deal of ingenuity to avoid, and even very competent playwrights sometimes fail. In *The Circle*, for instance, by Mr. Somerset Maugham, characters sit round and inform each other about facts in their family history of which, being close relations, none of them could well be ignorant.

Fiction, which still has the resource of Summary undisguised, has very little excuse for employing Summary badly disguised as Scene, when it needs to 'hark back to make up'. And yet in one form or another this fault still occurs. The device, for instance, of 'the tale within a tale' — not necessarily, but commonly a disaster — is not yet dead. It was one of the devices Jane Austen made fun of in her comic synopsis of a novel, designed to suit the tastes in fiction of the Prince Regent's librarian: 'Book to open with father and daughter conversing in long speeches, elegant language, and a tone of high, serious sentiment. The father induced, at his daughter's earnest request, to relate to her the past events of his life. Narrative to reach through the greater part of the first volume. . . .'

§ 2. FICTION MAY BE NEARLY ALL SCENE

The most vital part of a novel is always in the form of Scene, and Scene is the condition to which narrative seems always to aspire. In *Emma* Jane Austen seems to have tried to use the minimum amount of Summary, and very much less has been used by Henry James in *The Awkward Age*, and by Miss Compton-Burnett in all her novels.

But characters by Henry James and Miss Compton-Burnett do not talk like other people. In their speeches, often long, and usually unrealistic, they show a subtlety quite foreign to the stage — for which Henry James proved unfit, and for which

Miss Compton-Burnett has said she has no inclination. They are able to 'go behind' their characters, as Henry James would say. Older Drama could do this, in the soliloquy — modern prose drama on a picture-stage cannot do this — and it was this advance in realism, as much as anything else, that was the death of Drama as an art-form.

Miss Compton-Burnett's novels, moreover, abound in stage directions: if she makes her characters speak more than any other writer's, no other writer tells us more precisely how the people speak, or how they move when they speak.

They raise their eyebrows, stand squarely, look around, fall into open mirth (or into rather doubtful mirth); they give a yawn, draw themselves up, press their fingers to their brow, look faintly startled, or step impetuously forward. . . .

They may speak in a strident, self-confident voice; or in a colourless tone; a low, quick tone; an even tone; an open, considering tone; husky, languid tones; or a tender, almost shaken tone; on an urgent note; quietly; with a roguish eye; with an indulgent smile; or with a faint frown; with a touch of firmness, a touch of grimness, or a touch of earnestness; spacing their words; in a condoning manner; or even in a manner of saying what should be said, whether or no with hope of result. These examples have been picked, more or less at random, from one, only, of her novels; it is no exaggeration to say that her whole work would probably yield hundreds more.

Of course the way in which they say things modifies considerably what they say. This truth has been recognized by a very different writer when he says: 'In civilized life domestic hatred usually expresses itself by saying things which would appear quite harmless on paper (the *words* are not offensive) but in such a voice, or at such a moment, that they are not far short of a blow in the face.'[3] Miss Compton-Burnett will not allow an evil speech to appear harmless on paper — and that is one of her great and almost unique distinctions as a writer of dialogue.

The characters in *The Awkward Age*, who have more intangible things to convey, are even more subtle in their shades of expression. They faintly gasp, appreciatively sigh, ever so graciously smile, and protestingly moan their speeches. Now they are delightfully positive, now they speak with utter detachment, and now with an argumentative sharpness. Now they give little wails of baffled imagination, now their gaiety deepens, or they veer a little to indulgence. They can glare and grin and muse (all at once, so it would appear); they are indeed, as their creator often tells us, wonderful.

§3. SUMMARY IS NEEDED TO CONTROL THE TEMPO

A novel is not, like a statue or a picture or a building or a short lyric poem, all there at once — it is an experience that unfolds in time, like a play or a musical composition. A playwright or a composer can control the speed at which his works are performed, can at least indicate the speed he desires — and is able to provide for pauses. But the novelist writes for private reading, which may take place at any speed, and he has no reason to suppose that the end of a chapter will necessarily hold up the reader. He must therefore carefully keep such control as he can over the narrative tempo by structural means — for the tempo must be important in any art that cannot make an instantaneous effect.

'The object of a story is to be long,' wrote Stevenson, who was putting the process in its simplest terms, 'to fill up hours; the story-teller's art of writing is to water out by continual invention, historical and technical, and yet not seem to water; seem on the other hand to practise that same wit of conspicuous and declaratory condensation which is the proper art of writing. That is one thing in which my stories fail: I am always cutting the flesh off their bones.'[4]

It is not only that a story has to go on for a certain length of time — but that events in a story must occur at the proper place. In a child's composition the dénouement of a story is likely to take place in the first or second sentence, and more self-conscious writers do not always sufficiently prepare their events. Henry James took Mrs. Humphry Ward to task for this fault: 'I think your material suffers a little from the fact that the reader feels you approach your subject too *immediately*, show him its elements, the cards in your hands too bang off from the first page — so that a wait to begin to guess *what and whom the thing is going to be about* doesn't impose itself: the ante-chamber or two and the crooked corridor before he is already in the Presence.'[5]

It must generally be the work of Summary to guide the reader down the crooked corridor, or to entertain him in the ante-chambers — Scene is a more precious effect reserved for more important uses, and liable to debasement if put to servile tasks like these — it is also liable to become artificial or tedious.

Moreover the subject of a novel is often, in itself, a gradual process — the gradual formation, for example, or disintegration of a character. This is a subject almost impossible for a dramatist to handle: he must fasten on crucial incidents. Thus Racine, in the twelve-hour day of *Britannicus*, is able to show the first fatal steps by which Nero began his career of tyranny; and in the twelve-hour day of *Phèdre* he shows the final consequences of her long repressed passion. For a more complete unfolding of either process, Summary would have to give its aid. Even a rapid, if gradual, process like inebriation needs in part to be described by Summary. In *Savonarola Brown* Lucrezia Borgia hands a cup of wine to a gaoler, and he immediately becomes helplessly drunk — this instantaneous effect is not worthy of imitation; and there are too many dreary drinking scenes in dramatic literature, in which the process is as slow as in life, or slower; not the least dreary is that in *Guy Domvile*.

Henry James, in later life, was conscious of having got the time-scheme wrong in *Roderick Hudson*; of having gone too fast. 'Everything', he says, 'occurs . . . too punctually . . . Roderick's disintegration, a gradual process, and of which the exhibitional interest is exactly that it *is* gradual and occasional, and thereby traceable and watchable, swallows two years in a mouthful, proceeds quite *not* by years, but by weeks and months, and thus renders the whole view the disservice of appearing to present him as a morbidly special case . . . at the rate at which he falls to pieces, he seems to place himself beyond our understanding and our sympathy.'[6]

In an art that unfolds itself in time (and no metaphysical speculations about the nature of Time are here necessary — ordinary everyday time, that we measure with our watches, is meant) things must happen (or seem to happen) at the right time, and must take (or seem to take) the right time to happen.

'Life', says Maupassant, 'precipitates events, or drags them out indefinitely. Art consists, on the contrary, in making use of precautions and preparations, in arranging cleverly disguised transitions, in throwing the light on the essential happenings by skill in composition alone, and throwing all other happenings into suitable relief according to their importance.'[7]

In a novel in which Summary is almost totally lacking, time

sometimes seems to stand still. Miss Compton-Burnett's characters have to go away from their home circles at times: some of them teach or learn at schools or universities, others have one or another sort of 'London life'. But when we open one of her novels we are as certain to find them all at home as we are to find everyone in *Grandison* in the cedar-chamber. This is not a fault: the characters appear to feel that their family life goes on all the time, that there is no real escape from it, and that whatever they have done or suffered elsewhere is of little significance in comparison — this kind of continuity is indeed almost the worst terror of that kind of life.

For this reason, perhaps, she contents herself with very short passages of summary, short enough to be telling.

'Clement remained at the window after his brother had left him. He was to stand there several times in the next two months. At the end of them he came to the room where his sister was alone.'

Summary has also to be used to tell the history of happy people who have no history — happiness is seldom dramatic enough to be given in scenes. And yet one would be sorry to say that there is no room for happiness in fiction. People like reading about it, understandably. 'Why write about imaginary unhappiness,' they often say, 'when there is so much real unhappiness in the world?' It is a common plea of Circulating Library subscribers, and rather harder to take into account than their preference for 'Love without Sex'. But it expresses a feeling that even sophisticated novel-readers must share, if they are human. Sainte Beuve evidently shared it, and he must have included happiness in 'the good' that was too entirely absent from *Madame Bovary*. 'Is it, however, the office of art to wish not to console, to refuse to admit any element of gentleness and sweetness under colour of being more true?

For truth, if that were all that one were after, is not entirely
and necessarily on the side of evil, on the side of stupidity and
human perversity.'[8] The desire for some comfort from literature is not wholly to be mocked at and flouted — the scenes of
Levin's country life in *Anna Karenina* may cause what Henry
James calls a 'leak in its interest', but add immensely to the
geniality in which that book gains so much over Flaubert's
novel. Nor are the convalescences of Lucy Snow and of
Marianne Dashwood, in *Villette* and in *Sense and Sensibility*, the
least good things in those admirable books.

Even if it were not (in moderation) a good thing in itself in
fiction, happiness would earn a place there as a necessary
preparation for trouble. *O mors quam amara est memoria tua
homini pacem habenti in substantiis suis!* The novelist needs a little
space to show the man of substance in peace, and some passages
of summary in which to do it. Hardy has done this so well in
several chapters of *The Mayor of Casterbridge*, that it is a real
tragedy — we feel the decline and fall of Michael Henchard,
because we can believe that things could have continued to go
well with him, whereas Tess, with whom nothing could ever
have gone right, fails to move us so greatly. In life, as well as
in art, the persistently afflicted are more tedious than pitiful —
even more bored with than they are sorry for themselves.

In general, we may say of the happiness of fictional characters
very much what Proust says about their authors' happiness.
'As for happiness, it has almost only a single use, to make mis-
fortune possible. In happiness we must form very sweet and
very strong ties of confidence and attachment so that their
rupture may cause us that so precious heart-rending called mis-
fortune. If one had not been happy, were it only in prospect,
misfortunes would have been without cruelty, and, in consequence without fruit.'[9] Just as love is for fictional characters,

as Flaubert said it was for the artist, principally valuable as a source of suffering — its procreative function is so very unimportant in fiction.

Another history that has to be reported in summary (if it is reported at all) is the history of public events that have been going on while the characters in the novel have lived their private lives. This kind of summary is a temptation to the novelist: it is restful and easy to do, it fills up space, and makes his book look 'important'. But Jane Austen got on perfectly without mention of the Napoleonic wars, which must have been of interest to several characters in her novels: contemporary novelists are apt to make extensive reference to public events that are of much less importance to their characters — it is a satisfaction to the reader when he can catch them out in errors of chronology, he feels it serves them right.

The unpretentious news reels of Mr. John Dos Passos are probably as good a device as any for reporting news — if it must be done. Though the reader feels uncomfortably that an arbitrary selection of news items has been put in front of him, and that other selections would have served the author's purpose just as well — and this destroys completely the illusion of inevitability, so necessary for making us think that what we are reading is a work of art. However, they are so arranged that the reader can easily omit them, and get on with the story — this is, perhaps, a low sort of merit, but it is not altogether to be despised: too many excrescences on fiction cannot be spotted on a first reading — Dickens and Scott are very much better reading when we know them well enough to be able to skip.

It seems strange to mention Virginia Woolf in this company, but she had as a device a special use of summary designed to mark the passage of time, and to make pauses in her narrative.

She may have hoped that it would do for her novels something of what the chorus does in Greek tragedy — a suspension of time in timeless poetry, not altogether remote from the feelings and thoughts of the play. Unfortunately the central chapter in *To the Lighthouse*, and the passages about the waves in *The Waves* are failed poetry: this fact has been obscured because too many critics, unable to understand them, have not ventured to rate them at their proper worth.[10] Sensitive admirers of Virginia Woolf's work, who have been embarrassed by these passages, probably let their eyes travel very lightly over them on re-reading these books — and so they will be briefly held up, and the tempo will have been controlled, even if it has not happened quite in the way that the author intended.

§ 4 . FICTION THAT IS ALL SUMMARY

Fiction that is all Summary can hardly be called art at all. 'The art of fiction does not begin', writes Mr. Percy Lubbock, 'until the novelist thinks of his story as a matter to be *shown*, to be so exhibited that it will tell itself. To hand over to the reader the facts of the story as so much information — this is no more than to state the "argument" of the book, the groundwork upon which the novelist proceeds to create. The book is not a row of facts, it is a single image; the facts have no validity in themselves, they are nothing until they have been used.'[11]

Novelists sometimes are content to state the argument of a book, and to leave it at that, without even touching the difficult part of their art, indeed that part which alone deserves the name of art. Critics and readers are sometimes deceived into thinking that the resulting novels show a fine line or an artistic economy — whereas they are merely empty. Many short-story writers are forced by the exigence of space into this vice of synopsis writing; Mr. Somerset Maugham has not altogether escaped it. And the novels of Maurice Baring generally consist of little but groundwork, on which that novelist seldom built anything.

'The novelist who doesn't represent, and represent all the time is lost',[12] as Henry James says; he even speaks as if Summary ought to be ruled out altogether: 'Processes, periods, intervals, stages, degrees, connections may be easily enough and barely enough named, may be unconvincingly stated, in fiction, to the deep discredit of the writer, but it remains the very deuce to represent them.'[13] Perhaps it is not always necessary that processes, periods, intervals, stages, degrees, connections should be represented — if they are briefly stated in summary, and their consequences represented in scenes, the novelist may have done enough. The reader will not feel that he has been requested to take something on trust — 'the very death'[14] of the art of fiction.

As we have already seen, fiction is a rhetorical art, and seeks to communicate Feeling quite as much as Sense — and Feeling is not to be communicated in a bare summary. So that those who criticize adversely readers of fiction for being deeply moved by the woes of fictional characters while they are comparatively unmoved by accounts in a newspaper of an air crash, or a mine disaster, show a great insensitiveness to the power of words. St. Augustine (who himself used words magnificently) was temporarily forgetting their power when he blamed himself for weeping for Dido, and not for his sins. What is Hecuba to us? The mobled queen is everything that the poets of two thousand five hundred years have represented her to be — while yesterday's victims, whom war, dearth, age, agues, tyrannies, despair, law, chance, hath slain are less lamentable — *carent quia vate sacro.* At best, we can use our imaginations upon them, and ourselves become their poets: but Homer and

Vergil were better poets than we are. 'The facts are nothing [to us] until they have been used.'

'Representation' is of such importance that the reader feels particularly badly cheated if a big scene is avoided. Henry James rightly complains that in *The Bride of Lammermoor* there is a deviation of interest from the centre of the subject towards the frame — 'which is, so to speak, beautifully rich and curious' — because the central subject has never been represented in a scene. 'The situation represented is that Ravenswood loves Lucy Ashton through dire difficulty and danger, and that she in the same way loves him; but the relation so created between them is . . . never shown us as primarily taking place. It is shown only in its secondary, its confused and disfigured aspects — where, however, luckily, it is presented with great romantic good faith.'[15] We have never seen Edgar and Lucy in any way loving; we are merely told they love.

It is all the more unfortunate if a scene has been led up to, has been promised, as it were, to the reader, and then never takes place. A 'messenger's speech' is not at all sufficient, for in fiction, where we do not *see* the scene, the rules of classical decorum do not apply: Medea may kill her children before the people (i.e. the readers), though on the stage it would be revolting. Indeed she had better do so.

One would not like to say that nothing should ever be 'left to the imagination'. Fiction would then be severely limited; and George Moore was probably right in saying that 'there are scenes in life that cannot be written, even if they can be proved to have happened'[16] — though he may not be right in picking upon Willoughby's repentance in *Sense and Sensibility* as such a scene. Characters would lose in verisimilitude if the novelist lost his 'negative capability', and was not allowed to be in doubt about some of their motives — even the omniscient

Proust uses this power. And Henry James would then not be allowed his power of 'adumbration',[17] whereby he suggests more evil in *The Turn of the Screw*, and in one or two other stories, than is actually stated. The reader is encouraged to frighten himself thoroughly:

> *Like one, that on a lonesome road*
> *Doth walk in fear and dread,*
> *And having once turned round walks on,*
> *And turns no more his head . . .*

Nevertheless Henry James sometimes overdid 'adumbration'. We feel uneasy about the frightful apparition in the haunted room that killed Owen Wingrave. And when our fears have not been played upon, the adumbration is even less successful. We cannot at all believe in the something (unspecified, but dreadful) that Louisa Pallant tells a young man to discourage him from marrying her daughter.

'There may be such a state of mind brought about on the reader's part, I think, as a positive desire to take on trust', wrote Henry James, 'but that is only the final fruit of insidious proceedings, operative to a sublime end, on the author's side.'[18] When the reader sees through the insidiousness of the author's proceedings, trustfulness vanishes. It is not easy to trust the narrator in *The Figure in the Carpet* when he tries to make us believe that there was a cryptic *something* at the heart of Hugh Vereker's work, essential to its understanding, and unperceived even by the most intelligent critics. (It has become no easier to believe in this since people have busied themselves with the Figure in Henry James's carpet, and have propounded theories in which it is very difficult to believe.[19] We should remember George Corvick's words in this story: 'that if we had Shakespeare's own word for his being cryptic he would at once have accepted it. The case was altogether different — we had nothing but the word of Mr. Snooks.' We have not Henry James's own word for his work being cryptic.)

We are annoyed at things being left to our imagination, when we feel that the author's imagination has not worked hard enough: this suspicion, invalid in the case of Chekov himself, is only too valid in the case of most Chekovian short-story writers. Katherine Mansfield possibly entertained this suspicion about herself. 'What I chiefly admire in Jane Austen', she wrote, 'is that what she promises, she performs, i.e. if Sir T. is to arrive, we have his arrival at length, and it's excellent, and exceeds our expectations. This is rare; it is also my weakest point. Easy to see why. . . .'[20]

We are told that we should promise to perform virtuous actions when we intend to do them and are unlikely to be prevented (we give our future beneficiaries the pleasure of expectation, we further bind ourselves to do what we ought, and we acquire the extra merit of having fulfilled a promise — which is rightly denied to those mean people who say: 'I never make promises'). All this is no doubt applicable to fiction as well as to life, and we see that Jane Austen does indeed acquire an extra merit in this way — over and above the surpassing merit of Sir Thomas Bertram's return.

§ 5. SUMMARY INTO SCENE

At this stage it is time to hazard a definition of Summary and Scene. Scene is that part of a novel in which the novelist makes things happen under the reader's eyes. Summary is that part of a novel in which the novelist says that things are happening, or that they have happened — and sometimes there is a prophetic summary at the end of the book about things that will happen.

Scene cannot quite be equated with Dialogue, though Dialogue should probably not be used for purposes of Summary — the conversation between Sir Walter Raleigh and Sir Christopher Hatton shows what can happen if it is used in this way. There are, however, scenes that are not wholly in Dialogue — and various fusions of Summary and Scene.

For example, there is Scene in Indirect Speech — and since indirect narration is the form used, a great deal more can be said than what passed in dialogue between the characters. Nevertheless the novelist keeps near enough to Scene for the whole passage to have value as 'Representation'; he has 'represented' his processes, periods, intervals, stages, degrees, connections, or he has persuaded the reader that he has done so — which is nearly the same thing.

In the following passage from *The Spoils of Poynton*, far more is conveyed than a dialogue between Fleda and Mrs. Gereth could convey, but without much tiresome 'harking back to make up' — words and phrases of actual speech are reported, to give greater vividness.

'She hated the effacement to which English usage reduced the widowed mother; she had discoursed of it passionately to Fleda; contrasted it with the beautiful homage paid by other countries to women in that position, women no better than herself, whom she had seen acclaimed and enthroned, whom she had known and envied; made in short as little as possible a secret of the injury, the bitterness she found in it. The great wrong Owen had done her was not his "taking up" with Mona — that was disgusting, but it was a detail, an accidental form; it was his failure from the first to understand what it was to have a mother at all, to appreciate the beauty and sanctity of the character.

She was just his mother as his nose was his nose, and he had never had the least imagination or tenderness or gallantry about her. One's mother, gracious goodness, if one were the kind of fine young man one ought to be, the only kind Mrs. Gereth cared for, was a subject for poetry, for idolatry. . . .'

Flaubert, who needed a great deal of summary, wished nevertheless to represent everything. 'This should be six or seven pages at most, and without one *reflection* or one *analysis*,'[21] is one observation of his. Again he says: 'I persecute metaphors, and finally banish moral analyses.'[22] Yet by extreme skill in transition from Scene to Summary, by the insertion of vivid, photographic pictures to give life to narrative passages, he was able to use more Summary than appears to the casual reader. Moreover he will write what appears to be Scene in the imperfect tense ('they used to . . .'); another device which requires skill to use, but which used with his great skill enables him to convey a great deal of necessary information in such a way that it seems hardly separable from the happenings, which he produces before our eyes.

NOTES

1 *The Art of the Novel*, p. 321.
2 *The Critic*, II, p. 2.
3 C. S. Lewis, *The Screwtape Papers*, iii.
4 *The Letters of Robert Louis Stevenson*, ed. Sidney Colvin (London, 1900), II, p. 93.
5 *The Letters of Henry James*, ed. Percy Lubbock (1920), I, p. 330.
6 Loc. cit., p. 12.
7 Preface to *Pierre et Jean*.
8 *Causeries du Lundi*, XIII, 4 mai, 1857.
9 *Le Temps Retrouvé*, II, p. 65.
10 Cf. 'We all know that *The Waves* is a poem and a masterpiece, but we dare not read it; we cannot; we can no more read it than we can walk like flies, on the ceiling; we are too heavy, we sink, we fall. I say "we", but I make a very humble and tentative exception for myself! Having an insatiable passion for the sea, and having spent last winter with its waves coming in at my window, I fell in love at first sight with those matchless inter-chapters . . . and would not admit I could not read the book till, having read every page at least five times, I very nearly

SUMMARY

did understand it.' B. DE SÉLINCOURT, cit. DENYS THOMPSON, *Reading and Discrimination*, p. 106.

[11] *The Craft of Fiction*, p. 62.
[12] *The Art of the Novel*, p. 94.
[13] Ibid.
[14] Ibid., p. 224.
[15] Ibid., p. 68.
[16] *Avowals*, ch. 1.
[17] Loc. cit., p. 175.
[18] Ibid., p. 224.
[19] e.g. Mr. Edmund Wilson's theory about *The Turn of the Screw*, and Mr. Quentin Anderson's interpretation of *The Wings of the Dove*.
[20] *Journals*, January 2nd, 1922.
[21] *Correspondance*, II, p. 205.
[22] Ibid., III, p. 11, 10 mai, 1855.

I V

DIALOGUE

§ I. THE LATE APPEARANCE OF DIALOGUE

'We have seen', wrote George Saintsbury, of conversation in fiction, 'how very long it was before its powers and advantages were properly appreciated; how mere *récit* dominated fiction; and how, when the personages were allowed to speak, they were for the most part furnished only or mainly with harangues — like those with which the 'unmixed' historian used to endow his characters. That conversation is not merely a grand set-off to a story, but that it is an actual means of telling the story itself, seems to have been unconscionably and almost unintelligibly slow in occurring to men's minds; though in the actual story-telling of ordinary life by word of mouth it is, and always must have been, frequent enough.'[1]

Drama perhaps, in its great days, was monopolizing conversation. If fictitious characters wanted to talk, it was perhaps thought that the stage was there for that purpose — while, between the covers of a book, with no impatient audience to curb them, they could safely indulge in long set speeches.

Yet, though a late development, and a mark of growing sophistication in the art of the novel, there is nothing about conversation that makes it a particularly sophisticated taste. It was Alice who observed: 'What is the use of a book without pictures or conversations?' Fortunately she decided that it was of no use, and fell into her wonderful dream.

Some writers, and many readers have, however, felt and expressed some caution about conversation in fiction. Of course, like every other fictional device, it can be abused, it may become boring. Edith Wharton went so far as to maintain that only significant words should be said. 'The vital dialogue is that exchanged by characters whom their creator has really vitalized, and his instinct will be to record only the significant passages of their talk, in high relief against the narrative, and not uselessly embedded in it.'[2] This is an extreme, but an understandable, view.

Anthony Trollope has defined the place of conversation in the novel as well as anyone: he was no aesthetician, but he had great good sense.

'The dialogue is generally the most agreeable part of a novel; but it is only so as long as it tends in some way to the telling of the main story. It need not seem to be confined to that, but it should always have a tendency in that direction. The unconscious critical acumen of the reader is both just and severe. When a long dialogue on extraneous matter reaches his mind, he at once feels he is being cheated into taking something which he did not bargain to accept when he took up that novel. He does not at that moment require politics or philosophy, but he wants his story.'[3]

Too often we are given politics or philosophy, and with little relevance to the story, either because the novelist wishes to write propaganda for or against some point of view, or merely out of vanity — because he thinks he has something entertaining to say on these or other subjects. Sometimes it is out of laziness, for nothing is easier than writing dialogue on extraneous matters. It is the least exacting way of discussing art or thought, for as soon as a speaker gets into difficulties he can be interrupted, and all awkward questions can be left unanswered. The author remembers, conveniently, that his dialogue is intended to be dramatic and not Socratic, and he evades the obligations of philosophical dialogue just as he has ignored those of fiction.

This is not to say that fictional characters may not speak well, and on subjects of general interest — but it will be better if all the time their creator is asking himself, of all their utterances: 'does this further the plot?' or: 'does this reveal the speaker's character?' or: 'in what way does this tend to the telling of the main story?'

A resolution which André Gide noted in his journal is here in point. 'Don't go in for politics and hardly ever read the newspaper; but do not lose a chance of talking politics with no matter whom; it tells you nothing about public affairs, but it admirably informs you about people's characters.'[4]

The novelist can only give us stale information, and probably only second or third hand ideas about public affairs: what we ask him to give us, through the mouths of his people, is information about their characters.

It need not be the besetting sin of every fictional character that he shows off in conversation — a trait almost universal in Mr. Aldous Huxley's characters. There are people in real life who do not so show off — and they are sometimes found among people whose talk is polished and witty.

§3. THE MOST PLEASING FORM OF
DIALOGUE

Two novelists who abound in dialogue, Henry James and Miss Compton-Burnett, generally give us the highly polished conversation of very sophisticated and clever people. But their clever people are clever dramatically; their good things appear to proceed from the moment, and not from previous study. They cannot easily be detached from their context for quotation, and the whole context is brilliant, not merely a setting for a few flashy gems.

It was into such a world of civilized talk that Marivaux's heroine Marianne entered. 'It is certain', she said, 'that they had more wit than other people, and that I heard them saying excellent things; but they said them with so little effort, they were seeking so little for effect, it was so easy and uniform a tone of conversation that I might well have believed they were uttering complete commonplaces . . . Witty people are often accused of wishing to shine; oh there was no question of that here! And, as I have already said, if I had not had a little natural taste, a little feeling, I could have been mistaken, and I should have noticed nothing.'

It is this sort of circle that is most attractive in fiction. We do not only wish to read about characters who resemble the sort of people we should like to have for friends, we also like reading about silly, dishonest, rude and cruel people — but, if we are to listen to their converse, some of the same rules apply in fiction as in life. 'The company of clever, well-informed people, who have a great deal of conversation' is the best company.

As in real life, we will tolerate, and even enjoy the presence of some eccentrics and Malaprops — we can also appreciate the rustic simplicity of peasant speech — but the general level of conversation that we shall prefer will be that of educated people. So it is in the novels of Jane Austen and Henry James, in Stendhal and Proust and Tolstoy — so it is in the majority of the best modern novels, among others in those of Lawrence,

Virginia Woolf, Mr. Forster, Miss Compton-Burnett and Miss
Elizabeth Bowen, and in those of MM. Gide, Mauriac and
Camus.

§ 4 . THE VICE OF 'SCUDÉRYSME'

In easy and well-bred fictitious conversation, there is not any
ground for the uncomfortable suspicion that the characters
think each other very clever, and that the author is indirectly
complimenting himself through their mouths on his own cleverness. For all the cleverness they have is necessarily derived
from himself — apart from such quotations from other writers
as he allows them to let fall, and from such bits of out-of-the-
way knowledge as they evince. These are dragged in from his
arrière-boutique, or perhaps from the Encyclopaedia Britannica,
or other reference books.

The sin of self-praise, when thus practised by novelists, may
be called for convenience *Scudérysme*, after Mademoiselle de
Scudéry, who was so much addicted to it. Sainte Beuve writes
of her: 'In most of her dialogues, making her people talk, she
finds a way, after every good thing she gives them, to make the
one who replies say: "all you say is so well said" . . . Or, to use
a word she is fond of: "that is very well made out". This indirect compliment she pays herself recurs endlessly, and she is
inexhaustible in formulas for praising herself.'[5]

A more artful and self-conscious novelist, like Proust, is more
likely to make ironic use of the praise of one character's wit by
another character. The Duchesse de Guermantes is compli-
mented on her *bien rédigés* anecdotes, out of snobbery, by
characters who are sometimes too simple to understand them,
and are at any rate too simple to see how empty her wit is.
Madame Verdurin, who prides herself on having a *salon*,

exalts the pitiable wit of some of her guests, such as Cottard or Brichot. The same device is even applied below stairs, in the servants' hall of the narrator's home. For Proust wishes to show the paltriness of every kind of society, just as he wishes to show that every kind of love is a sickness. Of nearly every conversation in his book, we are to feel that it would be almost intolerable to take part in it — and yet it must be absorbingly interesting to read. This is perhaps the most difficult problem that dialogue raises for the novelist.

§ 5 . THE NEED FOR STYLIZATION

Words strain,
Crack and sometimes break, under the burden
Under the tension, slip, slide, perish,
Decay with imprecision, will not stay in place,
Will not stay still.

The written word is hard enough to control. Only by hard work and by re-writing, can we sometimes make words say what we mean, or an approximation to our meaning — only thus can we choose the right words, and place them in an elegant or witty order.

This cannot be done on the spur of the moment. Conversation in real life is therefore not often very good. The 'good talker' dominates it, like a professional soloist hired to perform with an amateur orchestra — and his phrasing is more competent than delicate. The civilized interchange of chamber music is sometimes found in drama or fiction, it is regretfully mentioned in some memoirs — but who has ever heard it? Conversation of that sort is often called a lost art, but it is quite likely that it never really existed — like the brilliance of Madame de Villeparisis's salon, which Proust tells us never existed except in her memoirs. When such conversation has been preserved in a record, it has naturally been recorded by the pen which selects, retouches and creates -- never by the merciless dicta-phone. As for the 'excellent things' that Marianne heard her friends saying, one may suspect that they contained a good deal of *marivaudage*. And the 'good talkers' — Dr. Johnson or Wilde — 'talk like a book': in a book one is more tolerant of their arrogance and vanity than one might have been in real life.

Moreover talkers have to tune up, and being tuned up they have to make an occasional concession to their audience. They must utter a few platitudes or nothings, refuse or accept cups of tea — it is selection, not strict verisimilitude that the recording Boswell will aim at — and we all know by now that Boswell was a great artist.

Selection, Arrangement, Stylization — it is these that turn talk into the art of conversation, and this is a literary art. Everything that people say is not interesting — but a fictional character must not bore the reader, even though it is his character to be a bore, and we may have to watch him boring other characters.

Very good criticism of fictional dialogue is that expressed by the Sultana in *Le Sopha*, by Crébillon fils. Almanzéi was telling his story, and used a large proportion of dialogue.

'This way of treating things', she said, 'is agreeable; it depicts the characters one puts on the stage better and more universally, but it is subject to some disadvantages. From wishing to get to the bottom of everything, or to seize every shade of expression, one risks falling into minutiae which are perhaps subtle, but which are not important enough to justify one's pausing at them, and one wears out the listener with tedious detail. To stop precisely where one should, is perhaps a more difficult thing than to create.'

'O if I knew how to omit,' wrote Stevenson, almost echoing the Sultana, 'I would ask no other knowledge. A man who knew how to omit would make an *Iliad* of a daily paper.'⁶

§6. THE BORE IN FICTION

Perhaps a man who knew how to omit could make a good comic character out of every bore of his acquaintance. This is unlikely: there is no reason to suppose that 'everyone is interesting' — this is one of the unproved dogmas of that sentimental philanthropy which for many people replaces religion, and it is no more credible than the related doctrines that everyone is really nice, or that everything is everyone's business.

Yet a man who knew how to omit and to combine, and where to stop, should be able to make at least one good comic character out of his experience; and it is from the bores that he would make it.

Nearly every great comic character is a 'flat' character — and in real life nearly every 'flat' character must be a bore. 'Flat' characters lack the charm of surprise, they are summed up in the stock phrase which they repeat at every entrance like a *leitmotiv*: it is for the novelist to see that their entrances are not too frequent, and that the *leitmotiv* is not allowed to drive us to distraction. As Macaulay said: 'It is a very hazardous experiment to attempt to make fun out of that which is the great cause of yawning, perpetual harping on the same topic. Sir Walter Scott was very fond of this device for exciting laughter: as witness Lady Margaret, and "His Sacred Majesty's disjune"; Claude Halcro, and Glorious John; Sir Dugald Dalgetty, and the Marischal College of Aberdeen; the Baillie, and his father, the deacon; old Trapbois, and "for a consideration". It answered, perhaps, once, for ten times that it failed.'[7] Life, alas, places even fewer restrictions than Scott upon the many people we know as 'flat' characters.

Moreover the bore in fiction has a dramatic function: in Trollope's words, his speech must, like that of every other character, 'tend in some way to the telling of the main story'. This gives him a prodigious advantage in interest over the bore in real life, who often seems only to interrupt the telling of the story.

It would need a detailed analysis of *Emma* to show how much of the story is in fact told by Miss Bates. Her knowledge of Highbury was, of course, incomparable, and she was not the sort of person to keep it to herself. In all innocence it was she who first furnished Mr. Knightley (and the reader) with a clue to the private understanding between her niece Jane Fairfax, and Frank Churchill.

Frank Churchill mentioned a rumour that Perry, the doctor, meant to set up a carriage: he believed that he had heard this from his stepmother, Mrs. Weston, who regularly wrote him news of Highbury. Mrs. Weston, however, had never heard of any such plan. Frank Churchill, guiltily aware that he must therefore owe the information to his clandestine correspondence with Jane Fairfax, tried to pass it off as something that he must have dreamed.

'Why, to own the truth,' cried Miss Bates, who had been trying in vain to be heard the last two minutes, 'if I must speak on this subject, there is no denying that Mr. Frank Churchill might have — I do not mean to say he did not dream it — I am sure I have sometimes the oddest dreams in the world — but if I am questioned about it, I must acknowledge that there was such an idea last spring; for Mrs. Perry herself mentioned it to my mother, and the Coles knew of it as well as ourselves — but it was quite a secret, known to nobody else, and only thought of about three days. Mrs. Perry was very anxious that he should have a carriage, and came to my mother in great spirits one morning because she thought she had prevailed. Jane, don't you remember grandmama's telling us of it when we got home? — I forget where we had been walking to — very likely to Randalls; yes, I think it was to Randalls. Mrs. Perry was always particularly fond of my mother — indeed I do not know who is not — and she had mentioned it to her in confidence; she had no objection to her telling us, of course, but it was not to go beyond; and, from that day to this, I never mentioned it to a soul that I know of. At the same time, I will not positively answer for my having never dropt a hint, because I know I do sometimes pop out a thing before I am aware. I am a talker, you know; I am rather a talker; and now and then I have let a thing escape me which I should not. I am not like Jane; I wish I were. I will answer for it *she* never betrayed the least thing in the world. Where is she? — Oh! just behind. Perfectly remember Mrs. Perry's coming — extraordinary dream indeed!'

What a thing Miss Bates has now popped out! What a thing she has let escape her! In all her rambling speech, the essential points are not lost. The Perrys' plan was known only to the Bates and the Coles — from 'the worthy Coles' it would not get to Mr. Frank Churchill. It was made known to Miss Bates and Jane Fairfax on their return from Mrs. Weston's house — therefore the unlikelihood of their having dropt a hint to her is much increased. Miss Bates ends, with unconscious irony, by praising her niece's discretion, just as she has begun with unconscious irony: 'if I must speak on this subject', when she has had to struggle for a hearing.

This speech is one of the many instances of that concealed art whereby Jane Austen reveals character and advances her story at the same time.

Sir William Lucas, in *Pride and Prejudice*, is only one of her minor bores; he is overshadowed by his wonderful son-in-law. Yet Sir William twice intervenes to set the story going. At his own house, he once forces Darcy to invite Elizabeth to dance — her refusal increases her value in Darcy's estimation, and when Miss Bingley accosts him, he is meditating on Elizabeth's fine eyes. At the Netherfield ball it was Sir William who put into Darcy's head the idea that Bingley and Jane Bennet were commonly thought to be attached to one another — giving Darcy the feeling that he ought to try to preserve his friend from an unfortunate connection. Darcy was too lofty to have observed the attachment for himself, and Sir William was perhaps the only person sufficiently insensitive to dare to tell him of it.

§ 7. THE SPOKEN WORD TRANSCENDED; JANE AUSTEN AND HENRY JAMES

The first part of *Pride and Prejudice* exhibits an even finer and more complex art; while Darcy and Elizabeth misunderstand each other the conversations between them, with the inevitable ambiguities — the words which are understood in one way by the speaker, in another by the hearer, and in a third way by the reader — are of a comic delicacy that is probably unique in literature. 'Cross answers and crooked questions' are common enough on the stage, and are an almost necessary element in farce — and at the opposite extreme, the subtle misunderstandings of Jamesian characters in such an empty novel as *The*

Sacred Fount, do little more than obscure the lack of meaning in the situation. The talk in the drawing-room at Netherfield shows a quite different skill.

'After playing some Italian songs, Miss Bingley varied the charm by a lively Scotch air; and soon afterwards Mr. Darcy, drawing near Elizabeth, said to her:

' "Do not you feel a great inclination, Miss Bennet, to seize such an opportunity of dancing a reel?"

'She smiled, but made no answer. He repeated the question, with some surprise at her silence.

' "Oh," said she, "I heard you before; but I could not immediately determine what to say in reply. You wanted me, I know, to say 'Yes', that you might have the pleasure of despising my taste; but I always delight in overthrowing those kind of schemes, and cheating a person of their premeditated contempt. I have, therefore, made up my mind to tell you that I do not want to dance a reel at all; and now despise me if you dare."

' "Indeed I do not dare."

'Elizabeth, having rather expected to affront him, was amazed at his gallantry, but there was a mixture of sweetness and archness in her manner which made it difficult for her to affront anybody, and Darcy had never been so bewitched by any woman as he was by her. He really believed, that were it not for the inferiority of her connections, he should be in some danger.

'Miss Bingley saw or suspected enough to be jealous. . . .'

In a very sensitive essay on *Pride and Prejudice,* Mr. Reuben Brower comments on the inadequacy of any possible stage rendering of the scene: we hear so much more with the mind's ear than any possible voice rendering could give. 'Elizabeth', he writes, 'hears his question as expressing "premeditated contempt" and scorn of her own taste. But from Mr. Darcy's next remark and the comment which follows it and from his repeating his question and showing "some surprise", we may hear in his request a tone expressive of some interest, perhaps only gallantry, perhaps, as Elizabeth later puts it, "somewhat of a friendlier nature". We could hear his "indeed I do not dare" as pure gallantry (Elizabeth's version) or as a sign of conventional "marriage intentions" (Miss Bingley's interpretation), if it were not for the nice reservation, "He believed, that were it not for the inferiority of her connections, he should be in some danger." We must hear the remark in a tone which includes this qualification.'[8]

Probably one should go even further than Mr. Brower: he seems to imply that while Mr. Darcy's frame of mind was complex, Elizabeth shifted from one simple point-of-view to another, and Miss Bingley's point-of-view remained steady. It is likely that there was a good deal of ambiguity in the ladies' minds. In consequence, in the mind's ear, the attentive reader does not only hear one voice, but a lovely polyphony of voices saying: 'Indeed I do not dare.'

In spite of the skilful irony of Henry Tilney's speeches in *Northanger Abbey*, and the complicated misunderstandings in *Emma* — it is only the plot of *Pride and Prejudice* that, in the earlier part of the book, enables Jane Austen to use this skill to perfection.

Though the misunderstandings between Henry James's characters are sometimes merely tiresome, yet he is the artist who has perhaps most subtly shown understanding between two people. The kind of communication between the two lovers at the beginning of *The Wings of the Dove* is another proof of the superiority of fiction over the drama. No two speaking voices could so entirely give the body and soul of the two people.

They are much in love, but they are kept apart because her

family wishes and even needs her to marry for money. They meet in Hyde Park, and, out of pride, in full view of Kate's aunt's house.

'Everything between our young couple moved today, in spite of their pauses, their margin, to a quicker measure — the quickness and anxiety playing lightning-like in the sultriness. Densher watched, decidedly as he had never done before.

' "And the fact you speak of holds you!"

' "Of course it holds me. It's a perpetual sound in my ears. It makes me ask myself if I've any right to personal happiness, any right to anything but to be as rich and overflowing, as smart and shining, as I can be made."

'Densher had a pause. "Oh you might by good luck have the personal happiness too."

'Her immediate answer to this was a silence like his own; after which she gave him straight in the face, but quite simply and quietly: "Darling!"

'It took him another moment; then he also was quiet and simple.

' "Will you settle it by our being married tomorrow — as we can, with perfect ease, civilly?"

' "Let us wait to arrange it," Kate presently replied. . . .

'He gave rather a glazed smile. "For young persons of a great distinction and a very high spirit we're a caution!"

' "Yes," she took it straight up; "we're hideously intelligent. But there's fun in it too — we must get our fun where we can." '

For young persons of a great distinction and a very high spirit they certainly are a caution, they are hideously intelligent — that is where they get most of their fun, and where the reader gets his. That is also why their situation is so moving — we are more moved by such a burst of feeling between persons whose communication is so intelligent and so witty. And in scenes

such as this we are shown the relation between them as primarily taking place — we are not told that Kate and Densher love,
as Scott tells us about Ravenswood and Lucy Ashton — we see
and feel them loving.

§8. VERBAL FLUX; HENRY JAMES AND BRADSHAW

Alas, it is only too easy to find passages where Henry James
incurs the strictures that the Sultana of *Le Sopha* pronounced
against Almanzéi. He wishes to get to the bottom of everything,
or to seize every shade of expression — and he falls, in consequence, into minutiae which are perhaps subtle, but which
are not important enough to justify one pausing at them, and he
wears out the reader with tedious detail.

Henry James was once very cross with someone who parodied
his style in a skit called: 'If Henry James had written Bradshaw.'
But he himself has shown us Charlotte and the Prince in *The
Golden Bowl* consulting a railway time-table.

'He could only keep his eyes on her. "And have you made
out the very train — ? "

' "The very one. Paddington — the 6.50 'in'. That gives
us oceans; we can dine, at the usual hour, at home; and as
Maggie will of course be in Eaton Square I hereby invite you."

'For a while he still but looked at her; it was a minute before
he spoke. "Thank you very much. With pleasure." To which
he in a moment added: "But the train for Gloucester?"

' "A local one — 11.22; with several stops, but doing it a
good deal, I forget how much, within the hour. So that we've
time. Only," she said, "we must employ our time."

'He roused himself as from the mere momentary spell of
her; he looked again at his watch while they moved back to

the door through which she had advanced. But he had also again questions and stops — all as for the mystery and the charm. "You looked it up — without my having asked you?"

‘ "Ah my dear," she laughed, "I've seen you with Bradshaw! It takes Anglo-Saxon blood." ’

By this time the exhausted reader wants to knock Charlotte's and the Prince's heads together.

A thesis might be written — and this is not the place to develop it — about the use of the railway time-table in fiction: the witty handling of it in *Zuleika Dobson*, the superb genius with which Proust has dealt with *le plus enivrant des romans d'amour, l'indicateur des chemins de fer*. We have seen Henry James with Bradshaw; for all his Anglo-Saxon blood, it was a fatal temptation to him.

§9 . TRIVIAL DIALOGUE

The over-elaboration of dialogue must not tempt us from the certitude that Selection, Arrangement and Stylization are necessary to dialogue in fiction. If we doubt this for a moment, we shall be easily convinced by our next glance into a book where the conversations are not characterized by Selection, Arrangement and Stylization. It would be invidious to choose a book — one picked at random from a station book-stall should do. We shall find talk that does not reveal character nor tell the story — speeches that might be changed round from one speaker to another without any loss. Whereas in the work of a great writer of dialogue — in Jane Austen, in much of Dickens, in Proust — we should always know who was speaking, even if the names were left out. It seems a thing to aim at, as a condition of achieving any distinction at all, that each character should have a 'voice' of his own. In too much modern fiction no individual voice is heard — though one or two novelists introduce a lisp or a stammer.

It is of course natural and necessary for characters, at times, to say things of little significance, in which no special voice can be heard. 'It is very warm today', or 'will you pass me the butter, please?' Such remarks may sometimes be necessary, in order to elicit more interesting replies from other characters.

How, asked Flaubert in despair, is one to make trivial dialogue which is *well written*?[9] His own answer was patient work, and careful art — and Stevenson's words suggest a course to take: 'O if I knew how to omit!' Omission can be learned.

The novel has here a great advantage over drama — not everything need be said, characters can be present without opening their mouths — we are not conscious of them standing round dumbly like people at a party who do not know the other guests. They can come and go without a reason being given for their exits and their entrances. If they eat or drink, light or throw away cigarettes, powder or blow their noses, they can perform these entirely uninteresting actions without our being informed of them — it would generally be better if we were not so informed; unfortunately some novelists (and many dramatists) seem to labour under the delusion that these entirely uninteresting actions are Action.

There is, however, Euphony to be considered, as well as Sense. Rhythm must be taken into account, and the right tempo must be maintained. Moreover the reader sometimes wants a pause. There is no way of creating a blank space in a book, as in Architecture, nor of writing a rest, as in Music. Perhaps there is nothing to do but to put in something entirely uninteresting.

Nor is it only trivial dialogue that is hard to write well. We do not, at tragic moments in our lives, commonly speak with tragic grandeur. We do not even write very well at such times. The letters that suicides leave behind them shock, more often than not, by their vulgarity — and yet the writers are doing much to prove the sincerity of the sentiments which they have so ill expressed; man can hardly do more.

Conrad writes of his pitiful heroine, in *The Secret Agent*: 'as so often happens in the lament of poor humanity, rich in suffering but indigent in words, the truth — the very cry of truth — was found in a worn and artificial shape picked up somewhere among the phrases of sham sentiment'.

Perhaps it is just as well that poor humanity, being so rich in suffering, should be indigent in words, otherwise we might suffer too much when we were told of other people's sufferings. Wordsworth was perhaps right when he said that we could bear more in verse than in prose, because of the 'small, but continual and regular impulses of pleasurable surprise from the metrical arrangement'.[10] Because these impulses were there lacking, he found 'the distressful parts of *Clarissa Harlowe*' too painful. He was evidently much of the opinion of the Rhyming Butler in *Lovers' Vows* (so well known to us from *Mansfield Park*) who said: 'Loss of innocence never sounds well except in verse.'

Tragic dialogue, then, is probably better when kept brief — and it is a case for recourse to Summary. 'Because in a novel comment is possible, it does not impoverish the feelings to reduce the language of the characters to that of ordinary speech. Their feelings can still be defined by description so that they are seen to be delicate and not coarse, precise and not vague'[11] —

nevertheless, for the sake of unity of tone and style, and of the readers' feelings, the less impoverished language there is, the better.

§11. HISTORICAL NOVELS

The beginning of *Ivanhoe* will serve as an object lesson. After a few pages of false history, a forest-scene is revealed in which two preposterous characters are discovered, Gurth the swine-herd, and Wamba the jester. Their fancy dress is described at some length, before they engage in a dreary and frigid piece of dialogue. The story is said to derive from an ancient chronicle, appropriately called *The Wardour Manuscript* — the language is that called 'Wardour Street' by Fowler, after that street 'Mainly occupied by dealers in antique and imitation-antique furniture'.

Here is some humorous dialogue between Gurth and Wamba.

' "How call you those grunting brutes running about on their four legs?" demanded Wamba.

' "Swine, fool, swine," said the herd, "every fool knows that."

' "And swine is good Saxon," said the Jester; "but how call you the sow when she is flayed, and drawn, and quartered, and hung up by the heels, like a traitor?"

' "Pork," answered the swineherd.

' "I am very glad every fool knows that too," said Wamba, "and pork, I think, is good Norman-French; and so when the brute lives, and is in the charge of a Saxon slave, she goes by her Saxon name; but becomes a Norman and is called pork, when she is carried to the Castle-hall to feast among the nobles; what dost thou think of this, friend Gurth, ha?"

' "It is but too true doctrine, friend Wamba, however it got into thy fool's pate." '

Scott was trying to write a language that should be intelligible rather than archaeologically correct, to give a vague mediaeval atmosphere, while avoiding the sort of antiquarian excesses committed by Strutt, who in *Queenhoo Hall* wrote such gibberish as this:

' "That same borel knight," said Hugh, "Benemp him how ye may, was a tall man and a brave — "

' "He a tall man!" cried Hob, "the foul fiend affray him, he is a carle, a princox. I'll tell ye, my hearts, this tall man, with his gay train as crank as a peacock's, passed my doors without giving me the good-day, or hansling a single cross with me for luck's sake."

' "Marry, that was a shrewd ill guise of his!" '

But Strutt was not the only example Scott had to learn from. He owns that Gurth's and Wamba's speech, having been in Anglo-Saxon, must here be translated — what then was to prevent him from translating it into the idiom of 1817? There was a precedent for this in *The Castle of Otranto*, where the dialogue is said to be translated out of Italian, and is genuine eighteenth-century English.

There are several ways in which tolerable historical dialogue has been written.

First, the dialogue of a past age may be faithfully reproduced — of which method Scott's border novels are the finest example. This is only possible when the age is not far distant.

Secondly, a kind of negative archaism can be used — the writer writes in the language of his own time, denying himself any words or references that are startlingly contemporary. Thackeray's *Esmond* is an example of this method.

Thirdly, a writer may straightforwardly use the language of his own time — as the Elizabethan dramatists did, whatever age they were representing — and as Horace Walpole did.

But one thing that is never endurable is the language of Wardour Street. Scott, who could tell a good story even in this abominable jargon, did much to make it popular. It did incalculable damage to the English language in the nineteenth century, and it is not dead yet; it has so completely permeated English letters, from translations of the Greek and Latin classics, down to advertisements, that many people are incapable of seeing anything objectionable in it. To those who have freed themselves from it, perhaps it is more repellant than it should be — perhaps one should be able to read *Ivanhoe* and *The Talisman* with pleasure in spite of it.

§ 12. DIALECT

In an age of universal literacy, when the whole country is overlaid by a stereotyped culture; when everyone reads the newspapers, listens to the wireless, and speaks or hears Board School English; then, for independence and freshness of speech we must go to people independent of this stereotyped culture, if they can be found — whether they would be said to be above it or below it.

From the practice of writers in the past, we may collect that much the same rules are here applicable as those we discerned in historical fiction.

A dialect may be faithfully reproduced — but this is only possible when it is not too far remote from 'standard English' to be readily understood.[12]

Or a writer may exercise an economy in his choice of words, omitting words that his rustic characters could not have used, and limiting himself to their syntactical forms.

The worst, and most common expedient, is to use a kind of

DIALOGUE

'Doric', of which it is as certain that it was never spoken in any place, as it is certain that 'Wardour Street' was never spoken in any age.

NOTES

[1] *History of the French Novel* (1919), p. 340.
[2] *A Backward Glance* (1934), p. 203.
[3] *An Autobiography* (1883), II, pp. 38-9.
[4] *Journal* (Americ-Edit., 1943), I, p. 54.
[5] *Causeries du Lundi*, 12 mai, 1851.
[6] *The Letters of Robert Louis Stevenson*, ed. Sidney Colvin (1900), I, p. 289.
[7] *Journal* for November 9th, 1832, cit. *The Life and Letters of Lord Macaulay* by SIR G. O. TREVELYAN, BT.
[8] *Scrutiny*, xiii, no. 2, pp. 101-2.
[9] *Correspondance* (Bibliothèque-Charpentier, 1920), II, p. 132.
[10] Preface to *Lyrical Ballads*. Even if we disagree with Wordsworth about *Clarissa*, yet it is surely sound criticism to object that some things in fiction may be too painful for us to bear. It is a sign of an author's power if he can make us bear a great deal — as Dickens makes us bear a great deal in the first part of *David Copperfield*. But it is possible to go too far, so far that a book cannot be read with any pleasure: I think the author of *Poil de Carotte* has gone too far.
[11] M. C. BRADBROOK, *Themes and Conventions of Elizabethan Tragedy* (Cambridge, 1935), p. 43.
[12] The faithful reproduction of a stammer or of an odd accent is to be deprecated, when the result is even more painful to the eye than the oddity represented could have been to the ear: e.g. Balzac's Baron de Nucingen. Henry James was wiser: 'The language spoken by M. Nioche was a singular compound, which may not here be reproduced in its integrity . . . The result, in the form in which he in all humility presented it, would be scarcely comprehensible to the reader, so that I have ventured to attempt for it some approximate notation.'

TERMS AND TOPICS

ACCIDENTS

'The number of people on this earth who die accidentally every day is considerable. But can we make a tile fall on the head of a principal character, or throw him under the wheels of a carriage, on the pretext that we must allow for accidents?'[1]

An accident makes a particularly unfortunate effect when the novelist has a very strong motive for getting rid of a character, and the reader must sometimes feel inclined to return a verdict of wilful murder against Hardy, for instance. Lord David Cecil's plea that Hardy aimed at exhibiting the helplessness of man in the grip of a rigid and hostile fate, is an eloquent plea for mercy — and it might avail if the accidents were less frequent and convenient. Characters must not die off like the brides of George Joseph Smith.

It is probably wiser to use an accident for the removal of a minor character — the results of his accidental death, and the reactions of the principal characters may be interesting: there seems no reason for a novelist to deny himself a moderate use of this theme.

AIM

'Mérimée once said to me something very true and sensitive: "In the little that I do, I should blush not to address myself to *my betters*, not to try to satisfy them." That is really the mark of every fine and sincere artist. One may make mistakes, but one must aim at satisfying one's equals (*pares*) or one's superiors, and not write for those who have less taste and wit than oneself; in a word, one must aim high, not low.'[2]

As well as analysing passages in terms of 'Sense, Tone, Feeling and Intention' we may also sometimes inquire what was the writer's Aim. His 'Tone' reflects his 'attitude to his listener',[3] his 'Aim' indicates his choice of listeners — not exactly the same thing.

BACKGROUND

'The setting of a novel is a thing of very small importance; the best is that which we know best, and not the most uncommon.'[4]

'Happy lovers are ready to put up with any kind of frame; they have in themselves the power of beautifying a desert. A luxuriant nature no doubt serves them better and enchants them; the grandeur of nature admired with another is the finest accompaniment of a noble love. But it is not right for the poet to insist upon it more than the lovers would be likely to do themselves.'[5]

'The material description of things and places is not, in the novel, so we understand it, description for description's sake. It is the means of transporting the reader into a certain setting favourable to the moral emotion which should spring from these things and places.'[6]

'For them [Elizabethan audiences] the actors were very plainly on the stage, but the characters might, half the time, be nowhere in particular. It was, for the dramatist of that day, a privilege akin to the novelist's, who may, if he chooses, detach characters, through page after page, from fixed surroundings . . . [Shakespeare] will always have, of course, as the novelist has, the whereabouts of his characters in mind, and casual allusion to it will crop out. There may also be the demands of the action for a house-door, a balcony, a tree or a cavern to be satisfied; but these things will have rather the utility of furniture than the value of scenery. And — this is the point — he need never give more attention to his play's background than he feels would be dramatically profitable. Moreover, he can give it — yet again as does the novelist — the exact sort of attention he chooses.'[7]

The picture-stage, which localized characters, robbed the dramatist of his privilege of leaving them nowhere in particular. This was probably the chief factor contributing to the ruin of drama — for it made soliloquy and formal speech appear absurd in prose drama. The novelist is unwise if he surrenders his privilege of delocalization.

Baggy Monsters

'A picture without composition slights its most precious chance for beauty . . . There may in its absence be life, incontestably, as "The Newcomes" has life, as "Les Trois Mousquetaires", as Tolstoi's "Peace and War", have it; but what do such large loose baggy monsters, with their queer elements of the accidental and the arbitrary, artistically *mean*? We have heard it maintained . . . that such things are "superior to art"; but we understand least of all what *that* may mean, and we look in vain for the artist, the divine explanatory genius, who will come to our aid and tell us. There is life and life, and as waste is only life sacrificed and thereby prevented from "counting", I delight in a deep-breathing economy and an organic form.'[8]

It has been argued that the analogy with a picture is misleading. 'A painting must be imagined in such a form that it establishes itself in existence, only in existence, at a glance; a novel, making its impression through the medium of language, can and does allow itself time for the last word to be absorbed by its reader.'⁹ It may be allowed that a novel's composition is not quite the same thing as that of a picture — but composition there must be, if it is to be a work of art; a symphony is not a success, if it is a 'baggy monster'.

See FLUID PUDDINGS.

BLASPHEMY

By derivation the word means simply 'injurious speaking', by usage it has come to mean 'injurious speaking about sacred subjects'. Writers who are also believers in a traditional religion, or who have at least been educated in such a belief, will be likely to use the word correctly. To them only sacred things are sacred. Other writers should use the word with caution — it might help them if they could obtain a copy of the list of subjects not to be spoken ill of, which is circulated in Greece by the Anti-Blasphemy Society, with the reminder that Blasphemy is an offence against God, a sign of bad manners, an abuse of the Greek language, and punishable by the civil code. This organization sometimes holds Anti-Blasphemy weeks in the provinces.

To speak of *Blasphemy* against Life, Love, Motherhood or any other human subject, is a sentimental abuse of a fine word. Mr. C. S. Lewis, in particular, ought to have known better than to censure the young woman who found Charissa suckling her babies in *The Faerie Queen* as revolting a figure as Error vomiting, for 'blasphemy against life and fertility'¹⁰ — for there is nothing essentially numinous about life and fertility. And the

Anglican bishop who once called hard words about the League of Nations 'blasphemy against the Holy Ghost', ought to have pointed out what he thought was the connection between the League and the third person of the Holy Trinity.

This is not to say that one cannot write or speak offensively about other than sacred subjects — there is probably no subject about which offensive words cannot be spoken or written. *Blasphemy*, however, is not then the word for the offence, and another should be found. Perhaps what is said is in bad MORAL TASTE (q.v.), or merely cynical, flippant, or vulgar.

CARNALITY

'She [Jane Austen] faces the facts, but they are not her facts, and her lapses of taste over carnality can be deplorable, no doubt because they arise from lack of feeling.'[11]

It would be easier to defend Jane Austen against a definite accusation — but her critics seldom hazard a definite accusation against her. We are left to wonder what lapses of taste Mr. Forster found in her work; we are at a loss to guess what meaning Mr. Stephen Spender could attach to the word 'vulgarity' when he applied it to her. They have not told us.

Jane Austen would probably answer that Mr. Forster was being 'missish'. He goes on to show much more sensibility than sense over her harmless jest, in a private letter to her sister, about the still-born child of Mrs. Hall of Sherborne. Jane Austen had lost sisters-in-law in childbed; its facts were her facts more than they can be any man's, except a man-midwife's.

She was far from lacking a sensitive awareness to the 'facts of life'. Her frank account of that scene at Lyme, when William Eliot shows signs of being sexually attracted by Anne, and this causes Captain Wentworth to look at her again with interest, may be contrasted with a far more 'missish' account in *Howard's End* of Margaret Schlegel's being attracted by a young waiter. And the 'almost animal emotion that consumed Marianne when she went up to London in search of Willoughby'[12] has been left out of Helen Schlegel, although her story requires something of the kind to be intelligible.

CLINICALISM

'Thus, in their desperate eagerness to hide nothing, these writers reveal things about their heroes that a man rarely learns about his fellows except from case-histories of their patients published by doctors. Is there room for surprise then, that these so-called heroes appear as so many clinical cases? It is not an equal who is offered to the reader's sympathy, but something like the insect whose entire behaviour the naturalist observes, behind a glass. The nature of the information we are given about him almost diverts us from regarding him as one of those beings like ourselves that we are in the habit of meeting in life and, in consequence, in literature. For, even when it has been given elevation by the author's talent, this information is still just like that which we are in the habit of receiving from specialized, one might say technical, research, carried out by scientists. Man is there necessarily treated as a thing; that is, without respect or shame. . . .

'It is best for us to know and ignore about fictional characters pretty much the same as we should be likely to know or ignore about them, if they were living people and we met them. A complete account degrades them and humiliates them. It robs everyone of the possibility of feeling for them that indispensable sympathy on which, for the most part, the illusion of fiction rests. We are invited to feel for a hero about whom we know

things it is impossible to know in life about anyone — unless we
are doctors and he is our patient, or unless he is a criminal, and
we are appointed to judge him. In a word, we know things
about him that no one must ever learn about us.'[13]

DOCUMENTATION

'The novel since Balzac', wrote the Goncourts, 'has nothing
left in common with what our fathers understood by the novel.
The actual novel is made with *documents*, related from life, or
heightened; just as history is made with written documents.
The historians are the narrators of the past, the novelists of the
present.'[14]

The originators of 'Mass-Observation' once said that their
findings ought to be helpful to novelists: the Goncourts were
precisely the sort of novelists who would have thought them
helpful — and their novels would have been even more lifeless
in consequence.

'They could never conceive that the happenings ought to
proceed from a character, and not a character from the happenings. They would have been capable, in a historical novel
about the Revolution, of grouping round an imaginary person
everything that resulted from a Marat or a Robespierre,
without understanding that, take away these real characters,
something would no doubt have happened, but not these same
things. They did not see that what happened to one person
would not have happened to another, because in the same situation their reactions would have been different. They practised
— and the old Goncourt even more than the two Goncourts —
the mutual independence of the man and the human anecdote:
it is what is called the literature of documentation. It is not
compatible with fiction. The same anecdotes, which in the

Journal have such an air of freshness and freedom, wedged into their novels acquire an indefinable awkwardness, and an air of having been forced.'[15]

DOVETAILING

'I have but done as the painters do — made compositions by dovetailing different sketches together.'[16]

The word *conflation* is sometimes used for the creation of fictional characters out of disparate observations. *Dovetailing*, though an even clumsier word, may help to describe the analogous construction of episodes or plots.

ESCAPISM

'Escapist literature is enervating when it leads one into wishful thinking about problems which must be faced. On the other hand, certain ageless books, marked by an understanding of the constant elements in human nature but concerned with problems no longer urgent, can be as restful as dreamless sleep after a day of heavy toil.'[17]

If 'Escapism' can ever be properly used as a term of reproach, it must mean 'a tendency to try to escape from that which we ought not to (or cannot) escape from'. On this definition, the novels of Charlotte Yonge are less 'escapist' now than ever they were. In 1853, if anyone had then spoken that horrible jargon, there might have been some sense in asking for 'socially conscious' novels, when the lot of the poor was so bad. Nowadays when the wealthier classes are compelled by taxation willy nilly to do their duty, and perhaps rather more than their duty, to their poorer brethren, and when everyone is 'socially conscious', we need to be reminded of the duties of private life.

There is no doubt that from these duties there are 'escapists' —
Mrs. Jellybys who think that charity begins in Borioboola-Gha.
And the journalist who did public penance in his column for
his share in the murder of Gandhi — because he happened to be
living when it occurred — could have found faults, no doubt,
that ought to have weighed much more heavily on his con-
science, and for which it would have been much less fun to
do appropriate penance, if he had been given to that kind of
self-examination that a reading of *The Heir of Redclyffe* might
have prompted.

FICELLE

Henry James described Maria Gostrey (in *The Ambassadors*)
and Henrietta Stackpole (in *The Portrait of a Lady*) as 'cases,
each, of the light *ficelle*, not of the true agent'.[18]

'Each of these persons is but wheels to the coach, neither
belongs to the body of that vehicle, or is for a moment accom-
modated with a seat inside. There the subject alone is en-
sconced, in the form of its "hero and heroine", and of the
privileged high officials, say, who ride with the king and
queen.'[19]

'Half the dramatist's art, as we well know — since if we don't
it's not the fault of the proofs that lie scattered about us — is
the use of *ficelles*; by which I mean in a deep dissimulation of
his dependence on them.'[20]

The 'ficelle' is a character belonging not to the 'subject' of
the novel, but to the 'treatment'.[21] Henrietta, for instance,
seems to be there as part of the author's 'provision for the
reader's amusement';[22] a part, he says, 'of my wonderful notion
of the lively'.[23]

FIGURES TO BE LET

'Annibale Caracci thought twelve figures sufficient for any story; he conceived that more would contribute to no end but to fill space; that they would be but cold spectators of the general action; or, to use his own expression, that they would be *figures to be let*.'[24]

Nobody would suggest taking the rule over, just as it stands, to the criticism of fiction, but the principle behind it is worth consideration. The term *figures to be let* could well be applied to FICELLES (q.v.) who do not somehow justify their presence.

'It is by the analogy that one art bears to another, that many things are ascertained, which either were but faintly seen, or, perhaps, would not have been discovered at all, if the inventor had not received the first hints from the practices of a sister art on a similar occasion.'[25]

FLUID PUDDINGS

'Don't let anyone persuade you . . . that strenuous selection and comparison are not the very essence of art, and that Form is [not] substance to that degree that there is absolutely no substance without it. Form alone *takes*, and holds and preserves, substance — saves it from the welter of helpless verbiage that we swim in as in a sea of tasteless tepid pudding, and that makes one ashamed of an art capable of such degradations. Tolstoi and D[ostoievsky] are fluid puddings, though not tasteless, because the amount of their own minds and souls in solution in the broth gives it savour and flavour, thanks to the strong rank quality of their genius and their experience. But there are all sorts of things to be said of them, and in particular that we see how great a vice is their lack of composition, their defiance of economy and architecture, directly they are emulated and imitated; *then*, as subjects of emulation, models, they quite give themselves away. There is nothing so deplorable as a work of art with a *leak* in its interest; and there is no such leak of interest as through commonness of form. Its opposite, the *found* (because the sought for) form is the absolute citadel and tabernacle of interest.'[26] See also BAGGY MONSTERS.

War and Peace seems to be held in such superstitious veneration by some people, that any suggestion that it is not self-evidently a perfect masterpiece, and the greatest novel in the world, is apt to be met with scorn and anger. It may be all that people say — those who cannot read Russian will never be quite certain what they have missed. But whatever it is, it does not look like a good model for an intending novelist (though no worse in itself for that). Anyone may, perhaps everyone should, sit down to write a *good* novel: no one should sit down to write a *great* novel.

FREEDOM

'It is a general prejudice, and has been for these sixteen hundred years, that arts and sciences cannot flourish under an absolute government; and that genius must necessarily be cramped where freedom is restrained. This sounds plausible, but it is false in fact. Mechanic arts, as agriculture, manufactures, etc., will indeed be discouraged where the profits and the property are, from the nature of the government, insecure. But why the despotism of a government should cramp the genius of a mathematician, an astronomer, a poet or an orator, I confess I never could discover. It may indeed deprive the poet or the orator of the liberty of treating certain subjects in the manner they could wish; but it leaves them subjects enough to exert genius upon, if they have it.'²⁷

'Heaven preserve you from a liberty of the press established by edict! Nothing contributes more to rendering a nation coarse, to destroying taste, and debasing eloquence and every sort of intellect. Do you know my definition of the *oratorical sublime*? It is the art of saying everything without being sent to the Bastille, in a country where it is forbidden to say anything. . . .'²⁸

The despotism that is really destructive to letters is one that imposes commands, not prohibitions — that orders the treatment of certain subjects, and in a certain manner.

GEOMETRY

'Really, universally, relations stop nowhere, and the exquisite problem of the artist is eternally but to draw, by a geometry of his own, the circle within which they shall happily appear to do so.'²⁹

We have to draw the line somewhere — we cannot treat all our characters' friends, business associates, distant connections, friends of the family, and friends of friends. Just as in real life we have to draw the line, and say: 'I will help you, but not your friends.'

In good fiction, characters move in a smaller circle than people in real life — they have only friends or habitual associates, and few acquaintances. It is unfortunate for fiction that contemporary life provides most of us with many acquaintances, and few friends or habitual associates.

Henry James drew the circle very tight. Edith Wharton once asked him: 'What was your idea in suspending the four principal characters in *The Golden Bowl* in the void? What sort of life did they lead when they were not watching each other, and fencing with each other? Why have you stripped them of all the *human fringes* we necessarily trail after us through life?'

She tells us that, after a pause of reflection, he answered in a disturbed voice: 'My dear — I didn't know I had!'[30]

IMITATIO CHRISTI

Here are the views of three eminent novelists on the *Imitation*.

'It is impossible not to be gripped by the *Imitation* which is to dogma what action is to thought . . . This book is a sure friend. It speaks to all passions, all difficulties, even those of this world; it resolves all objections, it is more eloquent than all preachers, for its voice is your own, that rises in your heart and that you hear in the soul. In short, it is the gospel translated, made appropriate to every age, imposed on every situation.'[31]

'Why, you dear creature — what a history that is in the Thos à Kempis book. The scheme of that book carried out would make the world the most wretched useless doting place of sojourn — there would be no manhood no love no tender ties of mother and child no use of intellect no trade or science — a set of selfish beings crawling about avoiding one another, and howling a perpetual miserere.'[32]

'It was written down by a hand that waited for the heart's prompting; it is the chronicle of a solitary, hidden anguish, struggle, trust and triumph — not written on velvet cushions to teach endurance to those who are treading with bleeding feet on the stones. And so it remains to all time a lasting record of human needs and human consolations: the voice of a brother who, ages ago, felt and suffered and renounced — in the cloister, perhaps, with serge gown and tonsured head, with much chanting and long fasts, and with a fashion of speech different from ours — but under the same silent far-off heavens, and with the same passionate desires, the same strivings, the same failures, the same weariness.'[33]

KNOWLEDGE OF MOTIVES

'. . . A character, to be living, must be conceived from some emotional unity. A character is not to be composed of scattered observations of human nature, but of parts which are felt together . . . A "Living" character is not necessarily "true to life". It is a person whom we can see and hear, whether he be true or false to human nature as we know it. What the creator of character needs is not so much knowledge of motives as keen sensibility; the dramatist need not understand people; but he must be exceptionally aware of them.'[34]

'I am not certain whether to know the world and to know human nature be not two distinct branches of knowledge, which while they may coexist in the same heart, yet either may exist with little or nothing of the other. Nay, in an average man of the world, his constant rubbing with it blunts that fine spiritual insight indispensable to the understanding of the essential in certain exceptional characters, whether evil ones or good. In a matter of some importance I have seen a girl wind an old lawyer about her little finger. Nor was it the dotage of senile love. Nothing of the sort. But he knew law better than he knew the girl's heart. Coke and Blackstone hardly shed so much light into obscure places as the Hebrew prophets. And who were they? Mostly recluses.'[35]

LITTERATURE ENGAGÉE

'Those who live by Letters, by the love of books and of study
. . . can grant for a moment a corner of their existence and lend
it to public thoughts and affairs — they ought to do so in urgent
cases; but, the emergency over, they have the full right to
return to their domain.

'This domain is a certain decent liberty, hard to define, but
very easy to feel, which means that one is not on any side, that
one is not always attacking or on the defence, that one seeks
for the good, the beautiful, the agreeable in more than one
place, that one's mind is like a window open to the sunbeam
that enters, to the passing bird, the smiling morning. . . .

'Those who believe that Truth is one not only in Ethics, but
also in Religion, Politics and everything, who believe they
possess this Truth and that they can demonstrate it to everyone
by clear and manifest signs, want all the time that literature
should never stray from the exact lines they have laid down
for her; but as in every age there is more than one sort of leading
spirits (not to speak of charlatans and imposters) who think
they are in possession of this unique and absolute truth, and are
equally anxious to impose it, and as these spirits are in opposi-
tion to each other, it follows that literature, that freedom of
poetic or scientific thought, pulled in different directions, would
be much embarrassed in the choice of an allegiance.'[36]

THE LOOKING-GLASS

'It sounds too fantastic for truth, but it is true, that the ulti-
mate defence of Elizabethan drama offered by many writers on
it, is that it holds up so faithful a glass to the "bustling, many-
sided life of that wonderful time".'[37]

Such writers Rupert Brooke calls 'wretched antiquarians'. There seems no reason why we should have any higher esteem for writers who want the novel to hold up a faithful glass to the 'bustling, many-sided life' of our own dolorous times.

Great novelists have, however, believed themselves to be holding up a glass. 'A novel', says Stendhal, 'is a mirror which goes along a high road. Sometimes it reflects the blue of the sky to your eyes, sometimes the mud and filth of the road.'[38] But he has to assume the presence of a man to hold the glass: 'And the man who carries the mirror on his back will be accused by you of being immoral! His mirror shows the filth, and you accuse the mirror! Rather blame the road where the mud is, or still more the road inspector who lets the water stagnate and the mud form.'

Yet if the glass reflects mud, that is not only the responsibility of the road inspector: the man who carries the glass is responsible, for he can turn it where he likes (it is ridiculous to think of it as strapped on his back). It may or may not be desirable and necessary to reflect mud: let us not evade responsibility, and say that we carry a glass, and cannot help ourselves.

THE MARVELLOUS

'A marvellous event is interesting in real life, simply because we know that it happened. In a fiction we know that it did not happen; and therefore it is interesting only as far as it is explained.'[39]

THE MILL-STONE

' "Politics", says the author, "is a stone tied to the neck of literature which sinks it in less than six months. Politics in the middle of imaginary interests, is a pistol shot in the middle of a concert. The noise is harrowing without being effective. It doesn't harmonize with the sound of any of the instruments. This politics is going to offend half the readers mortally, and to bore the other half who found it far more particularly and effectively in the morning paper. . . ."

' "If your people don't talk politics," rejoins the publisher, "they're no longer Frenchmen of 1830, and your book isn't a looking-glass any more, as you claim." '[40] But for this claim see THE LOOKING-GLASS.

'I hate politics. It is the cause of all I love being in danger, it threatens happiness, it disturbs me at my work. I believe with all my heart in art and literature. This faith is absolutely foreign to the preoccupations of politics.'[41]

MORAL TASTE

Jane Austen tells us that Henry Crawford had enough 'Moral Taste' to appreciate Fanny Price's affection for her brother William — in 'Principles' he must have been deplorably deficient, or he would not have eloped with a married woman. His sister Mary, on the other hand, though her want of 'Principles' was never proved, destroyed Edmund Bertram's affection by her disgusting lack of Moral Taste.

Some very bad characters, both in life and in fiction, have preserved their Moral Taste. Lovelace still worshipped Clarissa's moral grandeur, even while he was plotting to drag it in the dust — but the Présidente de Tourvel in *Les Liaisons Dangereuses* was pathetically mistaken in thinking that Valmont, her Lovelace, retained any love of virtue. And Proust tells us that Madame de Villeparisis, herself not at all a good character, spoke with exquisite sensibility about modesty and kindness — virtues which her parents had actually practised.

A novelist may be deficient in Principles, that is his own affair — but the values he consciously or unconsciously maintains will go wrong if he is deficient in Moral Taste. (No doubt Moral Taste will not long survive the total death of Principle, but that is a question for the moralist — so is the converse, for Moral Taste may be the first to go, as in Mary Crawford.) And it is surely by Moral Taste that we know 'what it feels like to be a man much better than ourselves' — though Mr. C. S. Lewis says that we do not know this.[42]

One of the many reasons why great fiction is difficult to write at present, lies in the almost universal decay of Moral Taste which always characterizes an irreligious age. People are not necessarily less moral, but there is no universal standard of Moral Taste — even among Principled persons — to which a writer can appeal.

NOTEBOOKS

'The literary instinct may be known by a man's keeping a small notebook in his waist-coat pocket, into which he jots down anything that strikes him, or any good thing he hears said, or a reference to any passage which he thinks will come in useful to him.'[43]

Samuel Butler had that instinct, and in consequence overloaded his novel with note-book material, *obiter dicta* about heredity, music, etc., which he had not been able to work off elsewhere. Such passages are both the best thing in the book, and its greatest defect — for they stand out like 'purple patches', and they intolerably hold up the interest. It is doubtful if notebooks are ever a safe quarry for a novelist: they did the Goncourts little good (see DOCUMENTATION).

Proust is decided on the subject: 'The man of letters envies the painter, he would like to make sketches, to take notes; he is lost if he does. But when he writes, there's not a gesture of his people, a twitch, an accent which has not been brought to his inspiration by his memory.'[44]

And memory does not serve the writer least well by its gaps and inaccuracies.

Maria Edgeworth is of the same opinion about the harmfulness of notebooks to the creative writer. (Of course the critic and the historian must have his 'Collections' — and without them the compilation, e.g. of such a book as the present, must be impossible.)

'I was averse to noting down,' she wrote, 'because I was conscious that it did better for me to keep the things in my head, if they suited my purpose; and if they did not, they would only encumber me. I knew that, when I wrote down, I put the thing out of my care, out of my head; and that, though it might be put by very safe, I should not know where to look for it; that the labour of looking over a note-book would never do when I was in the warmth and pleasure of inventing; that I should never recollect the facts or ideas at the right time, if I did not put them in my own way in my own head: that is, if I felt with hope or pleasure "that thought or that fact will be useful to me in such a character or story, of which I have now a faint idea," the same fact or thought would recur, I knew, when I wanted in right order for invention.'[45]

And again: 'I could never use notes in writing Dialogues; it would have been as impossible to me to get in the prepared good things at the right moment in the warmth of writing conversation, as it would be to lug them in in real conversation, perhaps more so — for I could not write dialogues at all without being at the time fully impressed with the characters, imagining myself each speaker, and that too fully engrosses the imagination to leave time for consulting note-books; the whole fairy vision would melt away, and the warmth and pleasure of invention be gone.'[46]

PARTICULARITY

'How to get over, how to escape from, the besotting *particularity* of fiction. "Roland approached the house; it had green doors and window blinds; and there was a scraper on the upper step." To hell with Roland and the scraper!'[47]

To hell, indeed, with the scraper, unless it serves some purpose in the story, e.g. to trip up Roland — and he establishes what D. H. Lawrence calls a 'lively relation'[48] with it.

It was this particularity that disgusted Paul Valéry with fiction. He could not induce himself to write: 'the Marquise arrived at nine', when she might equally well have been a Comtesse, and might equally well have arrived later. And yet it would not do to write: 'the titled lady arrived during the evening'.

A writer on another art has some help to give: 'I am ready to allow that some circumstances of minuteness and particularity frequently tend to give an air of truth to a piece, and to interest the spectator in an extraordinary manner. Such circumstances therefore cannot wholly be rejected; but if there be anything in the Art which requires peculiar nicety of discernment, it is the disposition of these minute circumstantial parts; which, according to the judgment employed in the choice, become so useful to truth, so injurious to grandeur.'[49]

See SUPERFLUOUS INFORMATION.

PERFECTION

'. . . Perfection is only one of the qualities of the work of art, and there is a quality superior to perfection itself, and that is life. Perfection can be considered as a full stop in the evolution of forms. Flesh is become marble, and that is the end . . . Perfection is then no longer the criterion according to which we shall judge a work of art. We shall ask of it beauty, a certain logical order, purity of language, originality of style and freedom of thought.'[50]

Nevertheless the idea of perfection in a work of art includes the presence of life, and the suggestion that a work would be better for the admission of more life at the cost of a little perfection is a dangerous one. For in a work of art Art is Life to that degree that there is absolutely no Life without it. Art alone *takes*, and holds and preserves, Life.

See also FLUID PUDDINGS.

PHYSICAL DESCRIPTION

If a novelist says that one of his characters is wise or good, it is his duty to make that wisdom or goodness apparent: but he may bestow physical beauty with a stroke of the pen, and ask us to take it on trust. As we cannot see fictional characters, and no one has ever described a face so as to compel the imagination, beauty is very much less important in fiction than it is in life. It is quite difficult, for instance, to understand why no one in Middlemarch was provoked at least to threaten to wring Rosamund's elegant neck — we have to pause, and to remember that she had a physical beauty not only sexually attractive, but capable of influencing her parents, her brother, and a woman like Dorothea. In *The Rise of Silas Lapham* by Henry James's friend, W. D. Howells, we are expected to be surprised at finding that the hero is attached to the plainer of two sisters — on the stage it might surprise, but in that novel the other choice would seem almost incredible.

Beauty can only be shown indirectly in fiction, in its effect on people — when this is sufficiently moving then the beauty of, e.g., Helen or of Lucien de Rubempré can move the reader at one remove. It may therefore be said that a great artist like Homer or Balzac can make a more beautiful face than a lesser writer can.

If beauty is to stir the imagination directly the novelist must probably borrow some help from the plastic arts: Odette de Crécy was like Botticelli's 'Jethro's daughter'; Milly, in *The Wings of the Dove*, was a Bronzino — and this is helpful, even to readers who get thereby no exact picture. (An extra-illustrated Proust would be a valuable piece of Grangerism.)

Voices are often said, vaguely, to be musical — but Madame de Mortsauf in *Le Lys dans la Vallée*, in whose voice were all the intonations of the paschal *O Filii et Filiae*, had surely the loveliest voice in fiction: it is hard to tolerate her rival the Marquise de Dudley — even though she was born 'in Lancashire, where women die of love'.

SOTTISIER

The collection of a *sottisier* is a conceited and dangerous hobby — it invites attention to our own unwary sayings; moreover the collector, in his zeal, is apt to put in remarks that are not, after all, so very silly, otherwise his collection will look too thin. This heading is therefore reserved for two remarks of a particularly sinister stupidity.

'Has anyone observed that no virgin, old or young, has ever produced a work, or anything?'[51]

'I hold Flaubert and Goncourt responsible for the repressions which followed the Commune, because they wrote not a single line to prevent them.'[52]

SUPERFLUOUS INFORMATION

'We meet [in Balzac] with artifices like those by which De Foe cheats us into forgetfulness of his true character. One of the best known is the insertion of superfluous bits of information, by way of entrapping his readers into the inference that they could only have been given because they were true. The snare is more worthy of a writer of begging-letters than of a genuine artist.'[53]

Sir Leslie Stephen instances as 'superfluous information' most of what Balzac tells us about the family history and homes of his characters, and all that he tells us about their armorial bearings.

Jane Austen was able to compress into fifty words the 'two handsome duodecimo pages' in the Baronetage devoted to the family of Elliot of Kellynch Hall, and found it unnecessary to tell us their arms and motto, though they would have known them (Sir Walter was proud of his supporters) and Mary Musgrove would have recognized them on Mr. William Elliot's carriage at Lyme, had not the panel been hidden by a greatcoat.

THE NOVELIST'S TOUCH

Mr. E. M. Forster, in his discussion of the 'flat' character, quotes Mr. Norman Douglas on 'the novelist's touch'.

'It consists, I should say, in a failure to realize the complexities of the ordinary human mind; it selects for literary purposes two or three facets of a man or woman, generally the most spectacular, and therefore useful ingredients of their character and disregards all the others . . . It follows that the novelist's touch argues, often logically, from a wrong premise: it takes what it likes and leaves the rest. The facts may be correct as far as they go but there are too few of them; what the author says may be true and yet by no means the truth. That is the novelist's touch. It falsifies life.'

Mr. Forster answers, perhaps too modestly, that the novelist's touch is bad in biography, for no human being is simple — but that in a novel it has its place. He suspects, however, on account of the greatness of Dickens, 'that there may be more in flatness than the severer critics admit'.[54]

And yet the novelist's touch may be good in biography, if it touch any character other than the subject. Nor is it a mere convenience in fiction. For fiction is not always about life as it is, but sometimes about life as it appears to such-and-such observers — even when the 'point-of-view' is not rigidly limited to what the narrator (David Copperfield, Mr. Overton or another) says and knows, or to the observations of a third-person, Henry Jamesian spectator.

And to everyone, in 'real' life, some human beings must appear as 'flat characters'. When we say that someone is a 'character', we almost always mean that he is a 'flat character'. And we say of some people that they have always been the same as they are now — which cannot be true, though it seems true to us. While we ourselves appear as 'flat characters' to some of our neighbours, whether we like it or not. We probably wish to appear 'flat' to many people with whom we do not care to be on terms of intimacy: we come out with our *leitmotiv* as soon as we meet them.

Fiction 'falsifies life', yes: but so does ordinary, everyday observation.

Once this principle is accepted, we shall have a slightly different approach to several problems, among others that of Obscenity. We know that everything can be done that is mentioned, for example, in the Kinsey report, and that every word can be said that is found in slang or dialect dictionaries. But many observers will never see or hear these things — there is no place for obscenity within the observation of Strether, or perhaps within that of Henry James — and therefore its omission from *The Ambassadors*, for example, is no more false to life than life itself.

Truth

What is Truth in Literature — for it is clearly not the same thing as historical truth? Perhaps the Cartesian definition is the best: 'whatever is clearly and distinctly apprehended is true'. And whatever Truth may be in Logic, in Literature Truth lies certainly in Coherence, and not in Correspondence with some outside set of facts.

It is always an artist's duty to tell the truth, it is never his duty to tell the whole truth; his function is to choose what truth is worth telling.

'Many truths are supremely boring. Half a man's talent lies in choosing out of the true that which can become poetic.'[55]

'To tell everything would be impossible, for it would need at least a volume a day, to enumerate the crowds of insignificant incidents that fill up our existence.'

'A choice, then, is forced upon us — which is the first blow to the theory of the whole truth.'[56]

'And for the authentical truth of either person or action, who (worth the respecting) will expect it in a poem, whose subject is not truth, but things like truth? Poor envious souls they are that cavil at truth's want in these natural fictions; material instruction, elegant and sententious excitation to virtue, and deflection from her contrary, being the soul, limbs, and limits of an authentical tragedy.'[57]

NOTES

[1] MAUPASSANT, preface to *Pierre et Jean*.
[2] SAINTE BEUVE, *Causeries du Lundi*, XI, Notes et Pensées cxlvi.
[3] I. A. RICHARDS, *Practical Criticism* (1929), p. 182.
[4] REMY DE GOURMONT, *Promenades littéraires*, IV (1920), art. 'Maupassant'.
[5] SAINTE BEUVE, *Causeries du Lundi*, 29 oct., 1849.
[6] EDMOND et JULES DE GONCOURT, *Journal*, 8 août, 1865.
[7] HARLEY GRANVILLE-BARKER, *Prefaces to Shakespeare* (Second Series), pp. 135-6.
[8] HENRY JAMES, *The Art of the Novel*, ed. R. P. Blackmur (1935), p. 84.
[9] STORM JAMESON, *The Writer's Situation* (1950), pp. 43-4.
[10] *The Allegory of Love*, p. 316.
[11] *Abinger Harvest*.
[12] GEORGE MOORE, *Conversations in Ebury Street*, chap. XVII.
[13] ROGER CAILLOIS, *Babel* (1945), p. 147.
[14] *Journal des Goncourts*, 24 oct., 1864.
[15] REMY DE GOURMONT, loc. cit., V, p. 61.
[16] JOHN GALT, *Literary Life*.
[17] MARGARET MARE and ALICIA PERCIVAL, *Victorian Best-Seller: the world of Charlotte M. Yonge*, p. 5.
[18] HENRY JAMES, loc. cit., p. 55.
[19] Ibid., p. 54.
[20] Ibid., p. 322.
[21] Ibid., p. 53.
[22] Ibid., p. 52.
[23] Ibid., p. 57.
[24] SIR JOSHUA REYNOLDS, *Discourses*, ed. Roger Fry (1905), pp. 88-9.
[25] Ibid., p. 209.
[26] *The Letters of Henry James*, ed. Percy Lubbock (1920), II, pp. 245-6.
[27] EARL OF CHESTERFIELD, *Letters*, ed. Bonamy Dobrée (1932), no. 1621.
[28] ABBÉ GALIANI, cit. SAINTE BEUVE, *Causeries du Lundi*, 15 oct., 1849.
[29] HENRY JAMES, *The Art of the Novel*, p. 5.
[30] Cit. SIMON NOWELL SMITH, *The Lesson of the Master* (1947), p. 112.
[31] BALZAC, *Madame de la Chanterie*.
[32] THACKERAY, *Letters and Private Papers*, ed. Gordon N. Ray (1945), II, p. 616.
[33] GEORGE ELIOT, *The Mill on the Floss*.
[34] T. S. ELIOT, *Selected Essays*, p. 132.
[35] HERMAN MELVILLE, *Billy Budd* (Edinburgh, 1924), pp. 44-5.
[36] SAINTE BEUVE, loc. cit., 13 oct., 1851.

TERMS AND TOPICS

[37] RUPERT BROOKE, *John Webster and the Elizabethan Drama* (1917), p. 57.

[38] *Le Rouge et le Noir*, II.

[39] SIR LESLIE STEPHEN, *Hours in a Library*, art. 'Balzac's novels'.

[40] STENDHAL, loc. cit.

[41] JULIEN GREEN, *Journal*, 4 avr., 1932.

[42] *A Preface to Paradise Lost* (1942), p. 98.

[43] *The Way of All Flesh*, chap. LXXIII.

[44] *Le Temps Retrouvé*, II, p. 54.

[45] *Chosen Letters*, ed. F. V. Barry (1931), p. 240.

[46] Ibid., p. 244.

[47] *The Letters of Robert Louis Stevenson*, ed. Sidney Colvin (1900), II, p. 299.

[48] *Phoenix* (1936), p. 529.

[49] SIR JOSHUA REYNOLDS, loc. cit., p. 73.

[50] REMY DE GOURMONT, loc. cit., IV, art. 'Les deux Flauberts'.

[51] *Journal des Goncourts*, 27 avr., 1862.

[52] J. P. SARTRE, *Situations*, II (1948), p. 13.

[53] SIR LESLIE STEPHEN, loc. cit.

[54] *Aspects of the Novel*, pp. 97-9.

[55] BALZAC, *Le Message*.

[56] MAUPASSANT, loc. cit.

[57] GEORGE CHAPMAN, dedication to *The Revenge of Bussy d'Ambois*.

APPENDIX

'INTIMATIONS OF IMMORTALITY'

The three authors here studied together have this in common, that we know a great deal about the sources of their inspiration. They have also this in common, that in the work of each of them *Bright shootes of everlastingnesse* are more than occasional accidents. Their work is built upon:

> *Those shadowy recollections*
> *Which, be they what they may,*
> *Are yet the fountain light of all our day,*
> *Are yet a master light of all our seeing.*

It may be useful to look at them, and to look at them together, even though no critical rule and no philosophical truth emerges: in their different ways, and with their greatly differing talents, they bear witness to something permanent in human nature — to our desire for our true country, which is not here.

For this desire, Christianity provides an explanation — but of these three writers Forrest Reid was defiantly unChristian, Proust apparently took little interest in the Christian explanation, and Alain-Fournier was only obscurely approaching it. Their evidence for the human desire for Heaven is all the more interesting, by reason of its independence.

This is a part of human experience much neglected in contemporary fiction. Secular novelists disapprove of people seeking those things which are above; religious novelists have developed a cult for 'evil', and those of their characters who have any spiritual perception (and these are often the most depraved) are usually more sensitive to smells rising from the bottomless pit, than to the clean airs of Heaven. This seems rather a pity — the worst thing about Hell is that it entails a final loss of Heaven. Alain-Fournier, Forrest Reid and Proust were certainly not such good Christians as Georges Bernanos, M. Mauriac and Mr. Graham Greene — perhaps they were more Christian novelists.

II. LE DOMAINE PERDU

Sologne is an out-of-the-way province, not far from Blois, not far from Orleans, not far from Bourges. It contains no remarkable beauty-spot, and no important architectural monument — it has the distinction of being the nearest approach to a desert in Central France. For Henri Alain-Fournier, whose home was first the school-house of Epineuil, and later that of La Chapelle d'Angillon, the fir woods of the Sologne, the small *châteaux* lurking among them, the tarns, the swamp, the desert, the hidden roads, the quiet villages, the horizons as wide as the sea, were the country of his soul.

Among his earliest letters to his friend Jacques Rivière, later his brother-in-law, are two nostalgic pictures of his province. His grandparents' house at La Chapelle d'Angillon calls back the smell of hot bread, brought home from the baker's at midday, of the cheese eaten as an afternoon snack, of his grandmother's cherry brandy, and all the wholesome and delicious smells of larder and garden, to Henri Fournier, a young exile in London, famished between the perpetual ham and jam of the English. An even dearer place to him is Nançay, the country of his dreams — all his wishes are summed up in a wish to spend the end of that summer there, the beginning of the shooting-season — and one day to be buried there.

'You get there, after five leagues' journey by hidden ways, in old carts. It's a country lost in the Sologne; the roads are all dry; all the way there are the yellow points of firs, fir woods on the neighbouring plains, horse-flies in the air, game that stops your path. There are always stories of smashed carts, floods, a horse bogged in the ford where they tried to water him.

'There Uncle Florent has a big general shop — a kind of world in itself "like *David Copperfield*". Behind it is a huge kitchen, like that of a farmhouse, where the family has its meals, in a jumble of children, dogs and guns. There are long days shooting in the woods or on the moors — luncheon, perhaps, with the gamekeeper of some exquisite small country house, buried in this wild landscape. You come home at evening, through the shop, busy by lamp-light, and drop off to sleep from exhaustion on a kitchen chair, waiting for dinner. Old faded photographs are passed round — school groups of one's father's boyhood.

'The dream of finding a friend who can thrill to your own past . . . I believe that is what one seeks, above all, in love . . .' Perhaps this dream was one of Henri Fournier's chief impulses towards authorship.

The *châteaux* of the Sologne, and their mysteries, whether based on fact or fable, were to Henri Fournier what Yorkshire legends had been to Emily Brontë. There was the little *château* hidden in the woods, where the sick young English milord had lived — he who courted their grandmother years ago — till the village lads beat him up for trying to steal away the prettiest girl in the neighbourhood, and he fled, by night, in a closed carriage. There was the deserted *château*, like the home of the Sleeping Beauty, discovered by Henri and Isabelle Fournier, and their parents, one summer day in childhood. La Varenne, visited from Nançay with their cousin Robert, all its elegance hidden away under dust-sheets — and the silent lake where there had been boats and water parties. There was the *château* seen from the train, marking their approach to home — 'at the *château*, Mother used to say to us: "Look at me, darling," and with her handkerchief she wiped some of the dirt of the train off our faces'.

When love came to him, he pictured the beloved as 'a young lady, under a white parasol, opening the gate of a *château*, some heavy afternoon in the country . . .' So he wrote to his friend, René Bichet. 'To picture "the Young Lady," one must have been a peasant child oneself; one must have waited endlessly, on June Thursdays, behind the railings of a courtyard — near the great white gates at the end of the walks, on the edge of the woods of the *château*.'

His love-story would seem adolescent and banal but for two things, it was a love that lasted his life, and it inspired a great work of art.

On June 1st, 1905, Ascension Day, Henri Fournier had just been to an art exhibition in the Petit Palais. As he went down the big, stone staircase, between four and five in the afternoon, he saw a tall girl just in front of him on the steps. She was fair — trying to give his sister an impression of her extraordinary beauty, he hit on the image of a spray of white lilac. He followed until he saw her enter a house in the Boulevard St Germain; on the succeeding days, as often as he could get away from his Lycée, he went and stood under the windows. One evening she looked out, and smiled.

Next day, Whitsunday, he went back early, dressed as a schoolboy, so as not to create a false impression. He hoped to catch her on her way to an early Mass, perhaps at St Germain des Prés. She appeared, in her brown cloak. '*Vous êtes belle*,' he said.

He followed her into a tram, and they both got down at St Germain des Prés. 'Will you forgive me?' he said, and she answered: 'What do you want with me, sir? I don't know you — leave me.'

'She can't mind my going to Mass,' he told himself; but he did not see her anywhere in church. At last he discovered a Mass being said in a chapel behind the High Altar — and the hat with the roses bowed over her folded hands. He gave his last sou to the woman who came round collecting chair-money; he was one sou short, for chairs were two sous each. It was the eleventh of the month, he would not get his pocket-money from his parents till the fifteenth — and he had been ruining himself in tram fares for the last ten days.

They walked out of church together. If she were to take the tram, all would be up with him — he could not follow, as he was penniless. But she crossed the road, and walked towards the Seine.

'Then begins the great, beautiful, strange, mysterious conversation . . . she listens now as if she had realized who I am; her blue eyes rest on me with sweetness, almost with friendship. It is as if we had understood, each of us, who we are . . . No more defences, no more embarrassment; we walk . . . as if we were alone in the world, as if this admirable Whitsunday morning had been, from all eternity, prepared for us two. . . .'

But to all he said, she could only answer in a sweet and hopeless tone: '*A quoi bon? A quoi bon?*' — lifting her head a little at the *b* as she let it out. Then she bowed her head, and bit her lip.

'I told her my plans, my hopes . . . also that I had begun to write, poems, that my friends liked. She smiled a little. Then I took courage and asked in my turn: "And you, won't you tell me your name?" '

In his mind he had called her Mélisands — from now on he called her by the name which she bears in his novel, Yvonne de Galais.

At the Invalides they parted.

'We must separate,' she said. 'We are two children, we've been mad . . . .' She asked him not to follow, and he leaned on the balustrade of the bridge and watched her go.

Next year he went at the same hour to the same place on Ascension Day, in case she came again. He was disappointed, and yet he felt, if he had tried hard enough, somehow his feeling would have compelled her to come. Surely he had attained his greatest spiritual height, when he had been allowed that vision?

'Your griefs, desires, resignations of that day were your true life, that is to say, your true happiness. You owed them to a past perhaps . . . of no importance,' wrote Jacques Rivière, sensibly enough.

But Henri Fournier could not give up his private religion of Yvonne de Galais — though at times he might blaspheme against it himself, or doubt it altogether, or give her irreverent nicknames, such as 'Amy Slim'.

'How bitter all this would be', he wrote to René Bichet, more than three years after that meeting, 'if I were not sure that one day, by the power of my longing for her, I shall get to the point where we are reunited, in the big room, "at home", on a late afternoon when she has been paying calls. And while I watch her take off her big cloak, and throw her gloves on the table, and look at me, we shall hear "the children" upstairs unpacking the big toy-box.' Already the image of the *Demoiselle* is connected with the hidden voices of children: 'Quick, now here, now, always — ' another natural image of Paradise, our first world.

The Easter after the meeting, he had told his sister Isabelle: 'I am dreaming of a long novel that revolves round her, in a setting which will be Epineuil and Nançay — she's found, lost, found again . . . It will be called *The Wedding Day* . . . The young man, perhaps, will run away on the evening of the marriage, out of fear of this too-beautiful thing given him, because he has understood that Paradise is not of this world. . . .

'I don't know . . . the book is in me; it is forming, it reveals itself little by little. . . .'

Yvonne de Galais is not only the ideal beloved, she is the 'objective correlative' — round her, and the search for her, he can bring to life all his childhood, and all his adored Sologne — and in her loss he can express that sense of loss that is inseparable from recollections of early childhood, that may have something to do with our original nostalgia for Eden, and may not be quite unconnected with our hopes of Heaven.

Already, reading *Tess of the d'Urbervilles*, he had been deeply moved by the 'happiness after *too much* pain, and after the crime' — the brief, impossible happiness of Angel Clare and Tess, before their inevitable parting.

From early youth he had meant to write a novel. 'First it was only me, me and me! Then little by little it became de-personalized, began to be no longer the novel everyone has in his head at eighteen,' so he writes to Jacques Rivière. He wants to begin, somehow, from Laforgue, and yet to write a novel — a novel in which dreams cross: an old fantasy comes back, and meets a departing vision. He wants to do without character and plot, and yet to remain a novelist. Perhaps his book will be a continual *va-et-vient* between dream and reality. 'I want to express the mystery of the unknown world that I desire . . . I want to make this personal world of mine live, the mysterious world of my desire, the new and faraway country of my heart

APPENDIX

... a life recalled with my past life, a countryside that the
actual countryside makes me desire.'

The departing vision is that of Yvonne de Galais — and the
Laforgue from whom he begins is the timid Laforgue, who
murmured:

> *Oh! qu'une d'elle-même, un beau soir, sût venir,*
> *Ne voyant que boire à mes lèvres et mourir.*

It is also the Laforgue of simple, poignant pictures:

> *Soeur faisait du crochet,*
> *Mère montait la lampe . . .*

And some of the melancholy of his Pierrot enters into the gipsy-
life of Frantz de Galais, and his companion Ganache.

But Yvonne de Galais married, and was lost to Fournier's
hopes — a loss to which he never quite resigned himself. 'I am
suffering from "desolation",' he wrote. 'My country no longer
wears the same face, reticent, mysterious and adorable. My
paths don't lead any more towards the country of that soul, a
country "curious" and mysterious like her. I've lost the
delicious and the bitter "fancies" that she woke in me, and
that were my whole life. Now I'm alone, at the centre of the
earth.'

He speaks mournfully of the festival that will never take
place — the wedding-day; he wants to write a book, or at least
a chapter of a book, that shall be called 'The End of Youth'.
His friend Jacques Rivière has married his sister Isabelle — and
the union of the two people nearest to him leaves him, at least
for a while, alone and in the cold.

Life offers him passing consolations, and he is not strong
enough to refuse them, though they only bring a worse desola-

tion — the pain of a man who longs for the purity of Eden, and whose life is not pure.

'Well, I've tried to live there, in Paris,' says Augustin Meaulnes in the novel, 'when I saw that everything was over and that it was not even worth the trouble any more, to look for the lost demesne . . . But a man who has once leapt into Paradise, how can he get used after it to the life of the rest of the world? What is happiness to others seemed mockery to me. And when one day I decided, sincerely and deliberately, to behave like other people, that day I piled up remorse enough for many a long day.'

Fournier's most personal confession is in a letter to René Bichet: 'At the deepest hour of the spring night, I am in the house of the fallen woman. I've slept in her bed: there's nothing more to say, I am going to go down the garden steps and to leave in the dark. But at the moment when it is time to end our secret interview, she holds me by the arm and falls back on the bed, saying: "Listen!" And a voice has burst out near us, in the garden; it mounts with a joy that raises, a purity that could disinfect this Hell. The nightingale is singing; and the woman smiles, like someone who has often seen the secret meeting of angels in a field, without talking about it, and reassures you as he goes across it with you — and she says; "he's there every night".'

The substitutes for Yvonne de Galais were one day to be conflated in the composite image of Valentine, the fiancée of Frantz de Galais, whom Meaulnes, in ignorance of her identity, made his mistress.

'She whom I met with her elder sister on a seat in a public garden, and as I spoke more gently to the elder, because the younger attracted me more, she said nothing and went away. . .' The dressmaker to whom Fournier sent his sister. The cast-off mistress who came back: 'she waited for me on a seat in the avenue, one night, two nights, ten nights. She said: "Time isn't long, when you're sure the person you're waiting for won't come."'

Henri Fournier was also to look for a substitute for Yvonne de Galais, further above her than Valentine had been below her. He found himself crying over 'a bad book about Bernadette and the pilgrims of Lourdes' (it was Huysmans's book). 'Lost companion, sister all-powerful, *turris eburnea, janua coeli.* Terrible queen, who smiled silently behind me as I read, and placed your hand on my shoulder with so much sweetness . . .' So he wrote to René Bichet; and he could not have forgotten another title of the Virgin: *hortus inclusus* or *le domaine mystérieux.* Two weeks later (after a visit to Lourdes) he wrote to Jacques Rivière, on the fourth anniversary of the apparition of Yvonne de Galais: 'Didn't I prove to myself the other day that every book led to some great triumph of the Virgin?' Yet so long as he lived he was never to find the lost demesne or its lady, on earth or in heaven, but only in his art. 'Perhaps,' Augustin Meaulnes was to say, 'when we die, perhaps Death alone will give us the key.'

When the experiences that went to the making of *Le Grand Meaulnes* are thus collected together, from Henri Fournier's letters to Jacques Rivière or to René Bichet, and from Madame Rivière's recollections of her brother, the novel seems almost their inevitable expression — but if it had not been for the novel, we should not have known which experiences to pick out as significant — a totally different novel of student life in Paris could very well be made from what is left over. Moreover his vocation as a novelist was known to him when he was very young, at an age when most future writers hope still that they are going to be poets — and Henri Fournier was already an artist when writing to his friends and talking to his sister.

'Novels without people, where the people are only the flux and reflux of life and its encounters.' This is one of his early notes. The chief people in *Le Grand Meaulnes* are only so far characterized as their functions require. Meaulnes is the big, silent boy who gets lost in the Sologne, and sees one December afternoon the tip of a grey turret above the fir trees: 'an extraordinary contentment uplifted him, a perfect and almost intoxicating tranquillity, the certitude that his end was now achieved, and that he had nothing but happiness now to expect'. He has taken his leap into Paradise. In hiding, he hears the voices of children talking of the mysterious wedding-feast of Frantz, at which they are to be masters of the ceremonies. He awakes to the unintelligible dialogue of Maloyau and Ganache, like that of a Shakespearian grave-digger and clown — they are going to reappear as Harlequin and Pierrot at the fancy-dress party, to which they invite him.

The chapters devoted to the strange wedding-feast are filled with an unearthly radiance. There is the dream-state of Meaulnes, come out of the surrounding cold into the warmth and light. Children are deputizing for the absent host, and most of the other guests are peaceable old people. Meaulnes was to say of them later: 'when one has committed some heavy, unpardonable offence, sometimes, in the midst of a great bitterness one thinks: "all the same, somewhere in the world there are people who would forgive me". One thinks of old people, of grandparents full of indulgence, who are convinced in advance that all you do is well done'. And the evening ends with the children sitting quietly, listening to Yvonne de Galais, the bridegroom's sister, playing old songs on the piano — a brown cloak thrown across her shoulders. Next morning, while the children were boating on the lake under a wintry sun, Meaulnes and Yvonne de Galais had the conversation that Henri Fournier had with the girl in the brown cloak on Whitsunday, by the side of the Seine.

But Frantz de Galais appears in the evening, in deep distress. The bride has failed to come with him, and the wedding will not take place. The feast breaks up in a hurry, and everyone goes home. Meaulnes gets a place in an old carriage, and falls asleep — in the morning he is set upon the road for Ste Agathe. He has, by sleeping, lost the track that leads to the hidden demesne — only a curious silk waistcoat, with mother of pearl buttons, part of his fancy dress, with which he has come away by mistake, remain to prove that it has not all been a dream.

François Seurel, the narrator, is the son of the school-teachers at Ste Agathe — as Henri Fournier was the son of the school-teachers at Epineuil. Meaulnes was their pupil and boarder, and François his closest companion. François is the uncharacterized narrator, distinguished only by lameness — a handicap which makes him fitter to share the adventure at one remove.

It is François who brings the book back from dream to reality after the wonderful adventure, and in the opening chapters he gives, with a few firm strokes, the setting of a school-house, in a Sologne village in winter, from which Meaulnes wandered by hazard into the mysterious wedding-feast. François keeps the level tone of a conscientious evangelist. 'The style to use', Henri Fournier had noted, 'is that of St. Matthew; *Christ's French*, as Laforgue said.'

When Meaulnes has gone to Paris in despair, it is François who discovers the way to the lost demesne. A school-friend speaks of a half-deserted property called Les Sablonnières. There, in the ruined chapel, he had seen a gravestone inscribed:

'INTIMATIONS OF IMMORTALITY'

Ci-gît le chevalier Galois,
fidèle à son Dieu, à son Roi, à sa Belle.

There's only a farm, and a small villa — the only inhabitants are an elderly retired officer and his daughter — there was a son, who had peculiar ideas. . . .

Les Sablonnières was near Vieux-Nançay where, like Henri Fournier's 'Oncle Florent', François Seurel's 'Oncle Florentin' kept the general shop. Of course the Galais are his customers, and Yvonne herself comes on the old horse Bélisaire to do her shopping.

She talks to François about his future career — she also would like to teach children: 'I wouldn't give them the desire to run all over the world, as I dare say you will, M. Seurel, when you are a school-master. I would teach them to find the happiness that is right beside them, though it doesn't seem to be . . . So, perhaps there's a big, mad boy looking for me at the end of the world, while I'm here in Mme Florentin's shop, under this lamp, with my old horse waiting for me at the door. If this boy saw me, he wouldn't believe it, would he?'·

'And perhaps I know that big, mad boy?' said François.

François went early next day on his bicycle, in search of Meaulnes, now passing his holidays with his mother at La Ferté d'Angillon. On the way he visited an old aunt — Henri Fournier's 'Tante Morenne' — who gave further authenticity to the mysterious wedding-feast, and attached it firmly to the real world. She had been there — she and her husband had been among the peaceable old people whom Meaulnes had met at dinner. On their way home they had met with the fugitive fiancée of Frantz de Galais. She was one of the daughters of a poor carpenter. 'She was convinced that so much happiness was not possible; that the young man was too young for her; that all the wonderful things he described to her were imaginary, and when at last Frantz came to fetch her, Valentine took fright. He was walking with her and her sister in the garden of the Archbishop's palace at Bourges, in spite of the cold and the strong wind. The young man, out of delicacy, and because he loved the younger sister, was full of attentions for the elder . . .' For a time the old woman took Valentine into her home, and then she went away to be a dressmaker in Paris, somewhere near Notre-Dame.

François finds Meaulnes about to set out on a long journey — he has a fault to repair, a fancied duty to help to find the fiancée of Frantz de Galais: 'when I discovered the nameless demesne, I was at a height at a degree of purity and perfection I shall never reach again. In death alone, as I once wrote to you, shall I perhaps find the beauty of that time once more'.

Oncle Florentin has organized a picnic, and Meaulnes and Yvonne de Galais are invited. Meaulnes learns from her of the ruin of Les Sablonnières, and of the poverty of her family — at the end of the day their last horse, old Bélisaire, is found to have lamed himself. It is a day of sadness and disappointment — but Meaulnes slips away from his friends at the end of the day, finds the road to Les Sablonnières, and offers marriage to Yvonne de Galais.

Frantz de Galais reappears on the evening of the marriage of Meaulnes and his sister. Frantz, like all the other characters in the book, but more than any, is a dream-figure, and more a symbol than a person. He is not a firmly conceived mediaeval symbol, standing for Weakness or Indecision — he is the symbolic figure of romantic literature, of which one cannot briefly say *what* he symbolizes, for that remains vague, and he is more potent in suggestion than symbolism. He owes a good deal to Hamlet.

He had first been seen outside Meaulnes's door, on the day after his arrival at the mysterious feast — a young man in a travelling-cloak, nervously whistling a sea-shanty, with a face of misery (surely Hamlet of Act V). He had next appeared at Ste Agathe, as a travelling gipsy with a bandaged head, in company with his faithful servant Ganache. There he had heard something of Meaulnes's mysterious adventure, for the other schoolboys were making fun of his strange absence. When they plotted to steal the map that Meaulnes was trying to construct of the way to the mysterious demesne, Frantz himself managed to steal it — and returned it to Meaulnes and François with a few corrections: by a schoolboy ritual (reminiscent of the cellarage scene) he made them swear to follow him, if he called on them for help. Before he left Ste Agathe he took off his bandages, revealing his identity to Meaulnes.

It was this promise, and a fault that he had to repair, that made Meaulnes hesitate to go to the newly found Yvonne de Galais — and on the evening of their marriage Frantz hooted from the edge of the wood; this time Meaulnes followed him.

The following chapters record the sickness of Yvonne, her recovery, her pregnancy and her death soon after her confinement — her body carried downstairs in the arms of François, because there was not room to carry down a coffin.

Henri Fournier had asked his sister's help: 'there are some very simple things, descriptions of familiar places . . . stories about little, everyday happenings that must be given absolutely clearly, with no admixture of symbolism . . . You would do this much better than me; you have a detailed memory, you knew it all with me, you would describe it all quite simply, as you recall it . . . And there are stories that you've told me that I want to use — like the day out by the Cher with the Groslins, which ended so badly with the accident to the horse that had been tethered too low, or Maria Bureau, whom a neighbour had to carry down dead in his arms because there was no room for a coffin to turn on the staircase.'

But Madame Rivière declines all the credit; it is her brother himself who achieved the purity and detachment for which he was striving, the faithful and humble rendering of small facts, and in the style of St. Matthew.

When Yvonne is dead, François goes through the papers in the house and finds a diary kept by Meaulnes. This contains some of the story of his attempts to live like other people in Paris. He falls in with Valentine, and she becomes his mistress — too late he discovers that he has not only betrayed Yvonne de Galais, but Frantz also; for he had never imagined that Valentine was the fugitive fiancée.

Valentine speaks of her former fiancé, and the promises he made her: 'we were to have had a house, like a cottage hidden in the country. It was quite ready, he said. We were to get there on the evening of our wedding-day, about this time — at night-fall, as if we were coming back from a long voyage. And on the way, and in the courtyard, and hidden in the trees, unknown children were to greet us, crying: "long live the bride!" '

There can be few novels of whose genesis so much is known. The happy appearance of a girl in a brown cloak as an 'objective correlative', the fusing of a calf-love, that became the love of a life-time, with Henri Fournier's love for Sologne: that is the history of *Le Grand Meaulnes*. But behind the nostalgia for *le domaine mystérieux* there is a very old nostalgia, once expressed by Henry Vaughan.

O how I long to travel back,
And tread again that ancient track!

'INTIMATIONS OF IMMORTALITY

That I might once more reach that plain
Where first I left my glorious train;
From whence th'enlightened Spirit sees
That shady City of Palm-trees.

III. THE RETREAT

The best thing ever said about Forrest Reid was said pro-
phetically by his friend, Mr. E. M. Forster, before the publication of any of his major work. *Following Darkness* had been
written, but with all the loose ends left that were to be tidied
up when the book was reissued as *Peter Waring*. *The Bracknels*[1]
and *The Spring Song* had been written, but they are both more
subtle in feeling and experience than their texture indicates:
their author was later to wish to rehandle them, as he had re-
handled *Following Darkness*. There was not yet anything of the
quality of *Apostate*, the autobiography, or of *Uncle Stephen*, his
masterpiece.

Mr. Forster likened Forrest Reid to Wordsworth, who spent
a lifetime in the recollection and expression of a vision that he
had received in his youth. 'He is always harking back to some
lonely garden or sombre grove, or to some deserted house whose
entrance is indeed narrow but whose passages stretch to infinity,
and when his genius gains the recognition that has so strangely
been withheld from it, he will be ranked with the artists who have
preferred to see life steadily rather than to see it whole, and who
have concentrated their regard upon a single point, a point
which, when rightly focused, may perhaps make all the surrounding landscape intelligible.'

In the opening lines of *Apostate* this is confirmed. 'The

[1] Later rewritten as *Denis Bracknel*.

primary impulse of the artist springs, I fancy, from discontent, and his art is a kind of crying for Elysium . . . Strangely different these Paradisian visions. For me it may be the Islands of the Blest "not shaken by winds nor ever wet with rain . . . where the clear air spreads without a cloud," for you the jewelled splendour of the New Jerusalem. Only in no case, I think, is it our own free creation. It is a country whose image was stamped upon our soul before we opened our eyes on earth, and all our life is little more than a trying to get back there, our art than a mapping of its mountains and streams.' He went on to say that he was speaking of a particular kind of art: Thackeray and Jane Austen loved this present world, and were not unique or even singular in this love.

In his dreams, he records, he visited the same spot night after night — he found himself on a grassy hill, sloping gently to the sea, and there he was waiting, never in vain, for what Corvo would have called 'the Divine Friend, much desired'. 'And presently, out from the leafy shadow he bounded into the sunlight. I saw him standing for a moment, his naked body the colour of pale amber against the dark background — a boy of about my own age, with eager parted lips and bright eyes . . . And from the moment I found myself on that hill-side I was happy. All my waking life, indeed, was blotted out. I had a sense of security, as if no doubt or trouble or fear could ever again reach me. It was as if I had come home; as if I were, after a long absence among strangers, once more among my own people. But the deepest well of happiness sprang from a sense of perfect communion with another being. Having tasted it, no earthly love could ever fill its place, and the memory of it was in my waking hours like a Fata Morgana, leading me hither and thither, wherever a faint reflection of it seemed for a moment to shine.'

A peculiar sympathy for the mysterious, because speechless, world of animals; a love for the drowsy, vague poetry of Poe, were also part of Reid's early, private world. Nor was this all: 'If you stand quite still in an ancient house, you will hear, even in broad daylight, strange sounds and murmurings. And so it was with me. I came on my mother's side, of a very old, perhaps too old a stock, one that had reached its prime four hundred years ago, and there were whisperings and promptings which when I was quite alone reached me out of the past. Very early I perceived that one's mind was swarming with ghosts.'

Apostate, he named himself, for the same reason that the name was given to Julian: he preferred the ancient gods. 'The Divine Friend, much desired' was later given the name of Hermes. A lovely statue of Hermes from Magna Graecia stood in Uncle Stephen's bedroom, blessed and blessing. 'He is the God of sleep and dreams,' Uncle Stephen explains. 'The last libation of the day was made to him — a kind of "now I lay me down to sleep" ceremony. The Greeks would have found Doctor Watts's poem quite appropriate:

> *With cheerful heart I close my eyes,*
> *Since Thou wilt not remove;*
> *And in the morning let me rise*
> *Rejoicing in Thy love.'*

Reid owned, in *Private Road*, that he did not quite know why the Divine Friend should be identified with Hermes. 'I knew little of Hermes. The Homeric Hymn did not fit in with my conception of him, and there seemed indeed little to be known. He was the guide of souls; he was a God of dreams, and also a boy God — a protector of boys, whose image was set up in the

corners of playgrounds and gymnasiums: there was the lovely
statue of Praxiteles.' There seem also to have been recollections of Homer: Hermes with his golden wand 'disguised as a
young man in the heyday of his youth and beauty with the
down just coming on his face' — who met Odysseus on his way
to Circe's palace, and gave him the saving herb, Moly. And he
seems, in *Uncle Stephen*, to have acquired some of the character-
istics of Asclepios, god of the dream oracle, who heals those who
sleep in his sanctuary.

His cult of Hermes he called: 'the acceptance of an imaginative symbol projected from an unknown spiritual energy. It is
not faith, because it will not bear the test of unhappiness: it
comes, rather, *with* happiness, and in the hour of loneliness and
loss would have no power to console ... Nevertheless, the
obstinacy with which it haunted my mind caused me to wonder
if it had not its origin in some universal spiritual force from
which Christianity and all religions had sprung'. He wrote to
a friend, who obtained for him from an unnamed source
what he quotes as 'the verdict of the Catholic church'.

'Your friend can find in his Hermes whatever spirit he likes
to evolve out of his hungers and desires, and this ideal of his
(in so far as it consorts with the ideals painted for us in the New
Testament) is no doubt the same spiritual ideal as you have
found in Christ, or rather one facet of it ... it is clear that
Christ is the fulfilment of all our earlier hopes and the reality of
our later dreams, so that there, in Christ, all religions touch
hands. . . .'

Forrest Reid took this answer to mean 'that to the Christian
mind I was clinging obstinately and wilfully to an outworn
creed, when all I had to do was to accept the light and the
truth'. Possibly further contact between him and the unnamed
author of 'the verdict of the Catholic church' might have

produced closer sympathy, though they could never have been of one mind — Reid might have found more reverence than he expected for the 'other Old Testament', that of Hellenism — and his unknown critic might have seen in Hermes a figure not so remote from the Christ revealed in some writings of the saints. 'The statement that I must see him as Christ would, it seemed to me, be exactly paralleled were I to insist that the Christian must see Christ as him,' Reid complained. The parallel is not so exact as he thought — but early Christians had seen Christ as Orpheus. Reid, however, preferred to think of Hermes rather as the likeness of a semi-divine figure — something like the archangel Raphael when he accompanied the boy Tobias.

Elysium, and Hermes its messenger, are at the heart of all his best work. He is surely describing himself in his interesting portrait of the novelist, Linton, in *Brian Westby*: 'In that first story, you see, he's only feeling his way — pretty blindly too — yet there is something even in it, which he's trying to express. It's not exactly a meaning, or an idea, or a message: at least it's not quite any of these, though in a way it's all three. I don't know what to call it; but it's there, and with each book it ought to become clearer. Mind you, I don't say it *does* . . . Nobody can do more than feel his way till he's acquired a method, learned his job, so to speak; and Linton was uncommonly slow in learning his. Besides, he often chose the wrong kind of subject; and in the beginning the writing itself was often bad. Still, after a fashion the books do fit together. I mean, he's got an ideal; and each of his books is an attempt to express it. So far as it *is* his book, that is to say, for the subject sometimes won't allow it to be. That's what I meant when I said he chose the wrong subjects. There's only the faintest glimmer of what he's really after in op. one, for instance; and in none even of the latest books, perhaps, is it there all the time. If he *could* bring it off, *could* produce it naked and complete — then I should think he might make a bonfire of the earlier things. They'd be only sketches and studies for the finished work . . . Which *may* mean — you know — and I can't help thinking really *does* mean, that he isn't a novelist at all . . . Or do you think that's to take him quite too seriously?'

In the autobiography, *Apostate*, and in *Uncle Stephen* and *The Retreat* Reid has surely brought it off, has produced his ideal naked and complete — and they are important works of art. It is, however, a good thing that he could not make a bonfire of all his earlier work, and there is later work that is of value for a further revelation of his vision, or for a comment on it. Nevertheless, it is probably better for his final reputation to leave out of the canon those books 'breaking the sequence', as he says, in which there is no other-worldliness. *Brian Westby* is the exception — for it seems to be an earthly story with a heavenly meaning.

Into *Following Darkness* not more than a hint of the supernatural entered. In *The Bracknels* — surely an expansion and rehandling of the theme treated by Henry James in *The Pupil* — the supernatural is evil, and destroys the boy-hero Denis, as it threatens to destroy Grif in *The Spring Song*.

Reid expected more popular success for *The Spring Song*: 'either the tale never found its true public, or the public disapproved of my method of presenting children'. Perhaps the writing was not good enough to let the book reach its true public: there is some embarrassingly bad verse, and much very indifferent prose. The author is dead, and the book cannot now be rewritten, as it deserves to be, but the Cinema might yet give new life to this beautiful fantasy of childhood — it remains, indeed, with the sympathetic reader as a series of images, because the vision is so greatly superior to the writing: the comic play scenes, made by the children out of a sentimental novel by their governess; Grif's quest for his dog, stolen by the circus people, and the loosing of all their stolen dogs; the mad organist and his hallucinations; and his death, in a thunder of music, in the blazing church.

Uncle Stephen was first a dream story: 'from beginning to end, it was composed in sleep — or perhaps I should say "lived", for I undoubtedly was Tom'. Its first title was '*My* Uncle's a Magician' — and the source of the dream is not beyond conjecture. The boy Forrest Reid had been supposed to have as his true ancestor a great-uncle — 'Henry of Ashchurch' — one of the mysterious relations who hovered tantalizingly in the unknown. He looked him up in the Burke of 1863, in the article 'Parr of Parr', and found that he had lived as a recluse, shut up among his treasures, at Lathwood Hall in Shropshire: 'He was many years a grand juror of that county, but declined to act as a magistrate from his love of retirement. He formed a valuable collection of paintings, coins, and medals, all of which, together with his library, were dispersed by auction after his decease in 1847.' And another Irish writer, Le Fanu, had written that haunting story of another eremitical uncle who was a wicked magician — *Uncle Silas*. While the predicament of Tom at the beginning of the story is that fancied for himself by almost every sentimental schoolboy in love with one of his fellows — that each should lose a parent, and the survivors should marry, and make them brothers.

Tom, now completely orphaned, is bored and misunderstood by his dull but well-meaning step-relations. Uncle Stephen projects a telepathic message to Tom, who goes to him in answer to his call, to his old, quiet house in the country. In the strange and beautiful magic that follows, out of Tom's desire for a young companion, and Uncle Stephen's wish that he could sometimes be Tom's contemporary — the years roll away for the old man, and he appears as his youthful self Philip, the boy who ran away from home. The magic gains in power, and Uncle Stephen is unable to resume his own personality. Tom's panic, Philip's realization that he is a Rip van Winkle, and the return of Uncle Stephen, are all worked out with imaginative matter-of-factness.

Philip, with his unearthly quality, is like a manifestation of Reid's tutelary spirit — and his appearance on the first occasion is in accordance with this character, a boy looking down through a screen of green leaves. He is to Tom — though human and often tiresome — something of 'the Divine Friend, much desired' of Reid's boyhood.

But to Reid's maturity 'the Divine Friend, much desired' must have begun to put on the resemblance of a son, a nephew or a spiritual heir. Hermes could not have seemed quite the same to Socrates as to Alcibiades — and even the Christian, who has once imagined himself as a child among the Five Thousand, and later as St. Peter or St. John, may come to imagine himself as St. Joseph or St. Simeon.

The epigraph is taken from *Job VI*. 8: 'O that I might have my request; and that God would grant me the thing that I long for!' Reid has not given the verse reference, probably because his prayer was not at all the prayer of Job, which goes on: 'Even that it would please God to destroy me; that he would let loose his hand and cut me off!' He was surely longing that his call could produce a young companion and spiritual son — fashioned, perhaps, like Tom, partly out of his own past; even as Philip, fashioned out of Uncle Stephen's past, came as a companion to Tom. He was surely praying for that fulfilment, expressed at the beginning of the book in lines from Wordsworth's *Michael* — lines which are repeated, altered into prose rhythm, at the end of the book.

> *They were as companions . . .*
> *Objects which the Shepherd loved before*
> *Were dearer now . . . From the Boy there came*
> *Feelings and emanations — things which were*
> *Light to the sun and music to the wind;*
> *And the old man's heart seemed born again.*

Uncle Stephen, that lovely fusion of the old man's vision and the young man's dream, could not fail to reach a part of its true public — though it cannot yet have found its way to many who might greatly love and admire it.

Reid's prayer was partly answered: Tom never left him again.

The Retreat, the second novel of the trilogy, shows Tom a few years earlier, when both his parents were alive. The beautiful opening pages are the transcript of a dream: the boy apprentice of an old magician is alone and frightened in a large bare room — there is a knocking at the door; trembling, the boy opens it and lets in a young fawn, with whom he escapes into a world of running water and green leaves. 'I saw in this', says Reid, 'a kind of symbolism, a pledge of the alliance I had formed from the beginning with the animal world.'

Another fragment, this time a scene from waking life, had for some years been haunting Reid because of its strangeness and beauty. Mr. E. M. Forster had taken him for a walk in London, and they had visited a small park. 'This park, I suspect, must originally have been part of, or adjoined, a graveyard, for all along one side of it was a broken wall composed of ancient tomb-stones, and now, at the hour of our visit, seated on each of these tomb-stones was a cat. The path was deserted, the cats were motionless, and in the stillness and the fading autumn light, the whole picture seemed drenched in a kind of sorcery, which, partly perhaps because I was so little prepared for it, created an immediate response in my imagination.'

Reid seems to have felt that the episode and the dream were part of the same book, before he knew what the book was to be. This is probably not an infrequent experience with authors; it is very like Gide's experience recorded in *Le Journal des Faux-Monnayeurs* — he was haunted by several scattered happenings. Gide allowed his former hero, Lafcadio, to serve as a temporary link — but discarded him before he wrote the novel. Reid also turned back to a former hero of his own. 'The first step was to ask myself — who would have had the dream? The second was — who would have encountered the cats? . . . The pregnant answer to both questions was "Tom" — Uncle Stephen's Tom . . . only it must be Tom, as I promptly realized, at an earlier stage in his development . . . Tom, in fact, at a transition period, when everything that happened to him should be new and mysterious, and wishes and fears change unaccountably and involuntarily into realities.'

Much of the book came out of 'real life': schoolboys, dogs and cats whom Reid had known, needed little alteration — a shop in Belfast, a Donizetti air he had himself sung as a boy, all were put in. But through all the realistic, Northern Ireland setting, Tom comes, trailing clouds of glory.

To him appears an angel, under the name of Gamelyn — very like the Raphael of Tobias. Gamelyn helps him to dodge the flaming sword, and to trespass in Eden. Eden is wild and overgrown, populated by many of the first created animals, who have eaten of the tree of Life. Tom talks to Dog, the original dog; he is mothered by Albatross, the original albatross; and he is dangerously wooed by the serpent — who puts forward quite a new story of the Fall. The Temptation had been a plot on the serpent's part, to get rid of Eva, who bored him, and to have Adam, whom he loved, all to himself again — all this is worked out with serpentine plausibility and exquisite humour.

Tom thinks of eating of the Tree of Life — he admits that he would like to live for ever.

'It only means for ever in that body,' the serpent said. 'It would be a foolish choice. You will live for ever as it is, though it will not always be the same life. But that is better — '

'Do you think so?' Tom pondered doubtfully.

'Much better,' said the serpent. 'How do you know that your present life will not become a burden to you? I could show you lives you have already lived, and I don't think you would wish to return to them.'

And again Tom was in the large bare room, hung with decaying tapestries, attending on the old alchemist, his master.

Young Tom, the third book of the trilogy, follows Tom back to schoolroom days: it is a pleasant book, full of animals, and connected with the other world by a young ghost — but it is not much more than an excuse for the author and his readers to enjoy more of Tom's company.

Brian Westby, which appeared between *Uncle Stephen* and *The Retreat*, is altogether more interesting and important.

It is a rationalization of the theme of 'the Divine Friend, much desired', and told as a purely realistic story. A novelist, Martin Linton, has gone to Northern Ireland for convalescence — he is not a little reminiscent of some of the writers in Henry James's stories, and his work is that of his creator. He finds a boy reading one of his own books — the boy is his own son. Years ago his wife had left him, not telling him that she was pregnant — she gave birth to a son, but concealed this fact when she asked Linton for a divorce; and when she remarried, the boy was brought up under his step-father's name, as Brian Westby. Linton slowly woos the friendship of the boy, and when they try the experiment of writing a story together, he places some sheets of his own composition in the boy's hands, and lets him read on, and find his father revealed by the style. One is reminded of the scene in *Les Faux-Monnayeurs*, in which Edouard charges Georges with stealing, by showing him a passage in his novel referring to a theft by another boy — but the original of this scene is rather to be found in the great closing pages of *Apostate* when the fellow-apprentice, in whom for a long time the dream friend seemed to be merged, was given Reid's intimate journal of all his thoughts and longings to read.

This is the writer in whose work M. Mauriac found 'le vide effroyable que creuse dans les êtres l'absence de Dieu'. It is an astonishing judgment, for Forrest Reid, if anyone, has painted that subject, proposed by the good bishop of Angoulême and Laure de Rastignac to the all unworthy Lucien de Rubempré — 'L'âme qui se souvient du ciel.'

IV. A NOTE ON PROUST

Marcel Proust disliked the English title given to the translation of his work: *Remembrance of Things Past*. It did not express the quest implied in his own title; and it seems that it was not only time but also Eternity that was the object of this quest.

This is often forgotten by his readers, and yet it is clearly expressed in his great words about the novelist's vocation.

'How happy the man would be, I thought, who could write such a book; what a task before him! To give an idea of it, it is from the highest and the most different arts that one must borrow analogies — for that writer (who moreover must make the most opposed facets of each character appear, so that its volume may be felt as that of a solid), must prepare his book meticulously, continually regrouping his forces, as for an offensive; he must endure it, like a fatigue; accept it, like a rule; construct it, like a church; follow it, like a diet . . . create it, like a world; without leaving those mysteries on one side which have probably no explanation except in other worlds, the presentiment of which is perhaps that which most moves us in life and in art.'[1]

He had reached the conclusion 'that we are in no wise free in the presence of a work of art, that we do not create it as we please but that it pre-exists in us and we are compelled as though it were a law of nature to discover it because it is at once hidden from us and necessary. But is not that discovery, which art may enable us to make, most precious to us, a discovery of that which for most of us remains for ever unknown, our true life, reality as we have ourselves felt it and which differs so much from that which we had believed that we are filled with delight when chance brings us an authentic revelation of it'.[2]

This vocation of the artist had, in music, been magnificently fulfilled by Vinteuil, in his great septet.

'This song, different from those of other singers, similar to all his own, where had Vinteuil learned, where had he heard it? Each artist seems thus to be the native of an unknown country, which he himself has forgotten . . . When all is said, Vinteuil, in his latest works, seemed to have drawn nearer to that unknown country . . . This lost country composers do not actually remember, but each of them remains all his life somehow attuned to it; he is wild with joy when he is singing the airs of

<hr/>

[1] T.R., II, pp. 329-40. Apart from this passage, all others are quoted from the translation by C. K. Scott Moncrieff and Stephen Hudson; but it is assumed that those who require references will want them for the French text.
[2] T.R., II, pp. 27-8.

his native land . . . .'[1] It was the mode in which Vinteuil 'heard' the universe, and expressed what he heard: 'This unknown quality of a unique world no other composer had ever made us see. . . .'[2]

To Swann, a phrase in the sonata of Vinteuil had held out 'an invitation to partake of intimate pleasures — of whose existence, before hearing it, he never dreamed, into which he felt that nothing but this phrase could initiate him; and he had been filled with love for it, as with a new and strange desire.

'With a slow and rhythmical movement it had led him here, there, everywhere, towards a state of happiness noble, unintelligible, yet clearly indicated.'[3]

To the narrator, a motif in the septet was 'an ineffable joy which seemed to come from Paradise';[4] he connected it with other 'starting-points, foundation-stones for the construction of a true life' — his impressions at the sight of the steeples of Martinville, or of a row of trees near Balbec.

'Two hypotheses', he says, 'suggest themselves in all important questions, questions of the truth of Art, of the truth of the Immortality of the Soul . . . It is not possible that a piece of sculpture, a piece of music which gives us an emotion which we feel to be more exalted, more pure, more true, does not correspond to some definite spiritual reality. It is surely symbolical of one, since it gives that impression of profundity and truth. Thus nothing resembled more closely than some such phrase of Vinteuil the peculiar pleasure which I had felt at certain moments in my life, when gazing, for instance, at the steeples of Martinville, or at certain trees along a road in Balbec. —'[5] The other hypothesis being that we magnify the importance of impressions which we are not able to analyse.

[1] P., II, pp. 74-5.   [2] Ibid., p. 235.   [3] S., I, p. 301.
[4] P., II, p. 79.   [5] Ibid., pp. 233-4.

There were 'privileged moments' in his life that Proust was able to analyse as no one else had analysed such moments — and the most famous is the wonderful moment of the *madeleine* and the cup of tea. His mother had persuaded him to have a cup of tea, and offered him a *madeleine*.

'And soon, mechanically, weary after a dull day with the prospect of a depressing morrow, I raised to my lips a spoonful of the tea in which I had soaked a morsel of the cake. No sooner had the warm liquid, and the crumbs with it, touched my palate than a shudder ran through my whole body, and I stopped, intent upon the extraordinary changes that were taking place. An exquisite pleasure had invaded my senses, detached, with no suggestion of its origin . . . Whence could it have come to me, this all-powerful joy? I was conscious that it was connected with the taste of the tea and the cake, but it infinitely transcended those savours . . . .'[1]

He tried again, and there was less power in the tea and the cake. He looked into his mind, and it told him nothing. Then he patiently cleared his mind of all other things.

'I place in position before my mind's eye the still recent taste of the first mouthful, and I feel something start within me, something that leaves its resting-place and attempts to rise, something that has been embedded like an anchor at a great depth; I do not yet know what it is but I can feel it mounting slowly; I can measure the resistance, I can hear the echo of great spaces traversed . . . And suddenly the memory returns.'

The narrator is in his Aunt Léonie's room at Combray.

'And just as the Japanese amuse themselves by filling a por-celain bowl with water and steeping in it little crumbs of paper which until then are without character or form, but, the

[1] S., I, p. 69.

moment they become wet, stretch themselves and bend, take on colour and distinctive shape, become flowers or houses or people, permanent and recognizable, so in that moment all the flowers in our garden and in M. Swann's park, and the water-lilies on the Vivonne and the good folk of the village and their little dwellings and the parish church and the whole of Combray and of its surroundings, taking their proper shapes and growing solid, sprang into being, town and gardens alike, from my cup of tea.'

The moment of the cup of tea was a moment in which a sense impression brought back the past with unusual power. Other 'privileged moments' were of this kind. Entering the courtyard of the Guermantes mansion the narrator had to step hurriedly out of the way of a carriage . . . 'Stepping backwards I stumbled against some unevenly placed paving-stones behind which there was a coach-house. As I recovered myself, one of my feet stepped on a flagstone nearer than the one next it. In that instant all my discouragement disappeared and I was possessed by the same felicity which at different moments of my life had given me the view of trees which seemed familiar during the drive round Balbec, the view of the belfries of Martinville, the savour of the madeleine dipped in my tea and so many of the other sensations of which I have spoken and which Vinteuil's last works seemed to synthesize . . . the sensation I had once felt on two uneven slabs in the Baptistery of St Mark had been given back to me.'[1]

On arriving at the musical-party given by the Princesse de Guermantes (formerly Madame Verdurin) the narrator had to wait for the end of an item in the programme. A servant brought him a glass of orangeade — and a noise the man made, knocking a spoon against a plate, caused in the narrator the

[1] T.R., II, pp. 7-9.

same sudden feeling of happiness as that in which the uneven paving-stones brought back Venice to him.

'This time my sensation was quite different, being that of heat accompanied by the smell of smoke tempered by the fresh air of a surrounding forest, and I realized that what appeared so pleasant was the identical group of trees I had found so tiresome to observe and describe when I was uncorking a bottle of beer in the railway carriage, and, in a sort of bewilderment, I believed for the moment, until I had collected myself, so similar was the sound of the spoon against the plate to that of the hammer of a railway employee who was doing something to the wheel of the carriage while the train was at a standstill facing the group of trees, that I was actually there.'[1]

On the same occasion the feel of a napkin brought back Balbec, and the sound of a water-pipe was like the scream of an excursion steamer there.

'Yes, if a memory, thanks to forgetfulness, has been unable to contract any tie, to forge any link between itself and the present, if it has remained in its own place, of its own date, if it has kept its distance, its isolation in the hollow of a valley or on the peak of a mountain, it makes us suddenly breathe an air new to us because it is an air we have formerly breathed, an air purer than that the poets have vainly called Paradisiacal, which offers that deep sense of renewal only because it has been breathed before, inasmuch as the true paradises are paradises we have lost.'[2]

And yet, though the cup of tea and the madeleine brought back Aunt Léonie's room at Combray; though the tapping of a spoon against a plate brought back the row of trees; though the feel of a napkin and the noise of a water-pipe brought back Balbec; though the uneven paving-stones brought back Venice;

[1] T.R., II, pp. 9-10.   [2] Ibid., p. 13.

and though many of these 'privileged moments' seemed to be synthesized in the later works of Vinteuil — this is not all. The peculiar joy which the trees at Balbec gave to the narrator remains unexplained, and so does his happiness at the sight of the towers of Martinville.

'In ascertaining and noting the shape of their spires, the changes of aspect, the sunny warmth of the surfaces, I felt that I was not penetrating to the full depth of my impression, that something more lay behind that mobility, that luminosity, something which they seemed at once to contain and to conceal. . . .'[1]

It seems at least a possibility that the pleasure given by the trees at Balbec, and by the towers at Martinville, since we are told that it was comparable with the pleasures of an involuntarily recalled memory, arose from the narrator's involuntary recollections of that unknown country which, as Wordsworth says, we forget at birth, but never wholly forget.

And perhaps we may refer to the narrator's joy at 'singing the airs of his native land', and neither to perversity, nor to a natural pleasure at seeing bits of a pattern fit together, the especial pleasure with which he finds a unity in his worldly experiences. It may be human wickedness which has caused the convergence of the different bits of the pattern, but the resulting unity may nevertheless reflect an other-worldly unity, remembered from that imperial palace whence he came.

There are several moments of this sort. For example, in the musical party at Madame Verdurin's, to which M. de Charlus invites the guests, *le petit clan* of the Verdurins and the world of Guermantes meet. Sodom and Gomorrah also shake hands: the efficient cause of the meeting is the friendship, now pure and exalted, between Mademoiselle Vinteuil and her friend —

[1] S., I, pp. 258-9.

the latter has laboriously deciphered Vinteuil's posthumous work: the final cause is the friendship between Charlus and Morel — Charlus hopes to get his young friend decorated. For the narrator Swann's way, in Mademoiselle Vinteuil, who came from Montjouvain on the way to Méséglise, here unites with the Guermantes way — and M. de Charlus connects both with Balbec.

(It would be tempting to compare Combray, crowned with its church of S. Hilaire, and Guermantes, on the Vivonne, with the Jerusalem and Babylon of patristic writers — so immortally a part of French thought since Pascal and Bossuet. The objection is that Proust would have delighted to make this comparison if he had intended it — he is not likely to have implied it in silence.)

Another occasion, in which Swann's way and the Guermantes way meet, is the *faire-part* sent out on the death of Marie-Antoinette d'Oloron, marquise de Cambremer.[1] She was Jupien's niece, adopted by M. de Charlus — therefore almost all the mediatized princes of Europe were put in mourning by her death. So also was the Comte de Méséglise — none other than Legrandin, of Combray and of Swann's way, the brother of Marie-Antoinette's mother-in-law, who had given himself this sham title. Swann himself is represented, for the Forchevilles' names are there — Odette de Forcheville, Swann's widow, was a cousin of Jupien. Balbec mourns, in the Cambremer family; Sodom is represented by Jupien, by M. de Charlus and by the widower; Gomorrah is represented by Odette, who also represents Mme Verdurin's little group.

All the threads are gathered together at the end of the book. Madame Verdurin is now the second Princesse de Guermantes; the Duc de Guermantes is, in old age, the lover of Odette de

---

[1] A.D., II, pp. 182ff.

Forcheville. Gilberte, daughter of Swann and Odette, is now widow of Robert de St Loup, and the intimate friend of Albertine's friend Andrée. Gilberte's daughter is daughter of Guermantes and Méséglise, of Sodom and Gomorrah. Already, in a previous volume, the narrator has visited Gilberte at Swann's house, Tansonville, and she has shown him that Swann's way and the Guermantes way are not geographically opposed as they had been in his childhood fancy — one can go to Guermantes by way of Méséglise.[1]

It is difficult not to see in this reception of the Princesse de Guermantes an illustration of 'the philosophy of Hermes that this visible world is but a picture of the invisible, wherein, as in a portrait, things are not truly but in equivocal shapes, as they counterfeit some real substance in that invisible fabrick'.

In short, *A la Recherche du Temps Perdu* appears to be less a Human than a Divine Comedy. The *Inferno* is terribly and unsparingly described — but the *Paradiso* is not completely absent. And though M. Mauriac has said that in all this vast novel God is absent, and it is true that no character in it troubles to perform what He commands — M. Mauriac is right in saying that the grandmother and mother of the narrator are pure and good on no supernatural principle — yet at least Swann and the narrator desire what He promises, and this is perhaps an even rarer sign of grace in the twentieth century. They not only have immortal longings, but they recognize that they have them.

[1] A.D., II, p. 206.

INDEX

ALAIN-FOURNIER, HENRI
  Le Grand Meaulnes, 123-38
Aldington, Richard, 42
Anderson, Quentin, 70
Archer, William, 32
Augustine, St., 16, 64
Austen, Jane, 17, 23-4, 26, 28, 55, 62,
    79, 86, 97, 140
  Emma, 55, 79-81, 83
  Mansfield Park, 18, 67, 88, 109-10
  Northanger Abbey, 83
  Persuasion, 74, 97-8, 115
  Pride and Prejudice, 81-3
  Sense and Sensibility, 18-19, 61, 65, 98

BALZAC, HONORÉ DE, 92, 99, 114-15,
    150
  Le Curé de Tours, 29
  Le Lys dans la Vallée, 114
  Madame de la Chanterie, 105, 118
  Le Message, 117, 119
Barrie, Sir J. M., 53
Baux, Cyril des, 52
Beach, Mrs. Hicks
  Amabel and Mary Verena, 39-41
Beerbohm, Sir Max
  Savonarola Brown, 59
  Zuleika Dobson, 86
Bernanos, Georges, 124
Bichet, René, 126, 128, 131-2
Blackstone, Sir William, 106
Bossuet, Jacques Bénigne, 157
Boswell, James, 77
Botticelli, Sandro, 114
Bowen, Elizabeth, 75
Bradbrook, M. C.
  *Themes and Conventions of Elizabethan
    Tragedy*, 88
Bradshaw, 85
Brontë, Charlotte, 22-3
Brontë, Emily, 125
  Wuthering Heights, 40, 49
Brontës, the, 22
Bronzino, Angelo, 114
Brooke, Rupert, 107-8, 118
Brower, Reuben, 82-3, 92
Browne, Sir Thomas, 158
Burke, Edmund, 21-2

Butler, Samuel
  The Way of All Flesh, 110, 116, 119

CAILLOIS, ROGER
  Babel, 98-9, 118
Camus, Albert, 75
Caracci, Annibale, 102
Carroll, Lewis
  Alice in Wonderland, 71
Cecil, Lord David
  Hardy the Novelist, 43-4, 52, 93
Chapman, George, 117-19
Chekov, Anton, 67
Chesterfield, Earl of, 103-4, 118
Coke, Sir Edward, 106
Coleridge, Samuel Taylor, 66
Compton-Burnett, I., 28, 55-6, 60, 73-5
  A Family and a Fortune, 60
  More Women Than Men, 56
Conrad, Joseph, 47, 52
  The Secret Agent, 88
Constant, Benjamin, 50
'Corvo', Baron, 140
Cowper, William, 48
Crébillon fils
  Le Sopha, 77-8, 85

DE FOE, DANIEL, 115
Descartes, René, 117
Dickens, Charles, 17-18, 28, 62, 86, 116
  Bleak House, 40, 49, 101
  David Copperfield, 38, 92, 116, 125
  Martin Chuzzlewit, 17-18, 33-4, 49
  The Old Curiosity Shop, 34
  The Pickwick Papers, 41-2
Donizetti, Gaetano, 148
Dostoievsky, Fyodor, 102
Douglas, Norman, 115-16
Dryden, John, 33
Dumas, Alexandre
  Les Trois Mousquetaires, 95

EDGEWORTH, MARIA, 111-12, 119
Eliot, George, 13, 28, 45
  Middlemarch, 13-14, 113-14
  The Mill on the Floss, 105-6, 118
Eliot, T. S., 32, 36, 38, 51-2, 76, 106,
    118, 128

INDEX

Eliot, T. S. (*cont.*)
  The Cocktail Party, 32
  Encyclopaedia Britannica, 75

FIELDING, HENRY, 29
  Tom Jones, 42
Flaubert, Gustave, 45, 47, 62, 69-70,
  87, 92, 115, 119
Forster, E. M., 75, 97, 118, 139, 147
  Aspects of the Novel, 115-16, 119
  Howard's End, 98
  The Longest Journey, 37
Fowler, H. W.
  Modern English Usage, 48, 51, 89

GALIANI, ABBÉ, 104, 118
Galsworthy, John, 39
Galt, John, 100, 118
Gandhi, 101
Gaskell, Elizabeth Cleghorn
  Cranford, 41
Gide, André, 21, 52, 73, 75, 92
  Les Faux-Monnayeurs, 150
  Journal des Faux-Monnayeurs, 118
Glanvill, Joseph, 37
Goethe
  Werther, 50
Goncourt, Edmond and Jules de, 94,
  99, 110, 115, 118-19
Gourmont, Remy de, 94, 99-100, 113,
  118-19
Granville-Barker, Harley, 94-5, 118
Green, Julien, 109, 118
Greene, Graham, 124

HARDY, THOMAS, 18, 23, 93
  Far From the Madding Crowd, 43-5
  The Mayor of Casterbridge, 23, 61
  Tess of the d'Urbervilles, 61, 129
  The Woodlanders, 23
  (*See also* Cecil, Lord David)
Heywood, Thomas, 36
Homer, 64, 114, 141-2
Howells, W. D.
  The Rise of Silas Lapham, 114
Hudson, Stephen, 151
Huxley, Aldous, 19-20, 27, 73
Huysmans, Joris-Karl
  Les Foules de Lourdes, 132

INCHBALD, ELIZABETH
  Lover's Vows, 88

JAMES, HENRY, 53, 58-9, 61, 64-9, 73-5,
  85, 95, 116, 118, 149
  The Ambassadors, 101, 117
  The American, 88
  The Art of the Novel, 69, 101, 104
  The Awkward Age, 55, 57
  The Figure in the Carpet, 66
  The Golden Bowl, 85-6, 104
  Guy Domville, 58
  Louisa Pallant, 66
  Owen Wingrave, 66
  The Portrait of a Lady, 101
  The Pupil, 144
  Roderick Hudson, 59
  The Sacred Fount, 81-2
  The Spoils of Poynton, 19, 30, 68-9
  The Turn of the Screw, 66
  What Maisie Knew, 38
  The Wings of the Dove, 20, 83-5
Jameson, Storm
  The Writer's Situation, 96, 118
Johnson, Samuel, 77
  Rasselas, 41-2
Joyce, James
  Ulysses, 29

KEMPIS, THOMAS À
  De Imitatione Christi, 105
Kinsey Report, the, 117

LACLOS, CHODERLOS DE
  Les Liaisons Dangereuses, 109
Laforgue, Jules, 129-30, 134
Lawrence, D. H., 11, 29, 42, 74, 112,
  119
Leavis, Q. D.
  Fiction and the Reading Public, 32, 51
Le Fanu, Sheridan
  Uncle Silas, 145
Lewis, C. S., 56, 69, 96, 110, 118-19
  A Preface to Paradise Lost, 34, 52
Liddell, Robert
  A Treatise on the Novel, 52
Locke, John, 46
Lubbock, Percy
  The Craft of Fiction, 63

MACAULAY, LORD, 78-9, 92
Mansfield, Katherine, 14, 25, 30, 47,
  67, 70
Marat, Jean Paul, 99

INDEX

INDEX